How to Master Your
KARMA

A Practical Guide to Living a Prosperous Life

How to Master Your
KARMA

Doctor Lynn Wylnn

Copyright © 2024 by Doctor Lynn Wylnn

All rights reserved. No part of this book may be reproduced, distributed, or transmitted in any form or by any means, including photocopying, recording, or other electronic or mechanical methods, without the prior written permission of the author, except in the case of brief quotations embodied in critical reviews and certain other noncommercial uses permitted by copyright law.

ISBN (paperback): 979-8-218-35398-8
ISBN (ebook): 979-8-218-35399-5

Book design and production by www.AuthorSuccess.com

Printed in the United States of America

To my many students who have supported my teaching and graciously thanked me with numerous emails, letters, and hugs.

Contents

Preface	ix
Introduction	1
Chapter One: How Did We Get Here?	5
Chapter Two: What Does it All Mean?	11
Chapter Three: Time Gates	14
Chapter Four: Karma Particles	16
Chapter Five: What is Karma?	18
Chapter Six: Make Punja not Papa	26
Chapter Seven: We are Here to Prosper	29
Chapter Eight: The Four Aims Leading to Prosperity	34
Chapter Nine: What is Your Karma?	46
Chapter Ten: What is Your Karma?	53
Chapter Eleven: Now You Have Your D-GAP	75
Chapter Twelve: Maya—the Illusion (what is real?)	77
Chapter Thirteen: The Four Blocks	82
Chapter Fourteen: The Troublesome Four	85
Chapter Fifteen: The Nine Obstacles	91
Chapter Sixteen: Nine Qualities and Characteristics to Develop	107
Chapter Seventeen: Soul Walking — The pathway of prosperity with a purpose	128
Chapter Eighteen: The Energy of Prosperity—RECAP	133
Chapter Nineteen: The Nidhi—the container that holds the treasures of life	138
Chapter Twenty: The Nidhis The treasures of life	143
Chapter Twenty-One: Where are the Nidhis?	171
Glossary of Karmic Words and Terms	179

Preface

The preface of a book is the place where the story begins, and mine begins with being abandoned as a child, then adopted, and then ending up on a small island off the coast of Maine.

I grew up in a small, isolated fishing village. The winters were very long and harsh. Survival meant we all worked together to ensure the survival of the island tribe. Only some homes had indoor plumbing. My first school was a two-room shed with no running water or central heat. We used outhouses and wood burning stoves.

Growing up in this environment always made me feel out of place. I tried to adapt and fit into the village, but I kept wondering how I ended up in this remote part of the world. Even if you don't feel isolated or alienated, I believe everyone, at some point in their lives, asks the important questions: Who am I? What am I doing here? What does this all mean? These questions are life's greatest drives. We all want to find meaning and purpose.

Karma teaches that we are born into a place with parents and family, as well as friends who give us the most expedient way to work our karma. We just need to be aware and use these opportunities to discover how to do so. The island life was all about survival and endurance. It meant hard work and instilled in me a work ethic of strength, determination, and appreciation for nature and the simple things in life.

I had a nagging feeling that there was something more beyond this fishing village and that the island was an incubator from which I would hatch one day and fly away. I wasn't sure where I would go, so I did what everyone did. I went to work.

Like most island girls, I married young and had children. By the age of twenty-five, I was divorced and on welfare with only a high school diploma. But I did have a strong will and deep determination, so I found a way to go back to school at the University of Maine, leaving the island and moving to the city.

However, mastering my life didn't come right away. Along with raising two children as a single mother, I was met with many perils. A string of poor choices in men, getting fired, sexual advances from bosses, discrimination in the workplace, having my heart broken, losing my business to unscrupulous partners, and a diagnosis with cancer, not to mention the lonely, stressful, and fearful nights and days.

What I realized as I began to explore the world and grow in awareness was that there were many opportunities to discover within myself why I was here and what was this crazy life all about. Life is full of obstacles. We can let them imprison us or we can develop characteristics that liberate us and allow us to succeed. What I discovered is a formula for success. By learning to walk the soulful path, I found a practical guide to living a healthy, happy, and successful life. But most of all, I discovered how to be true to myself; for that is the ultimate success in life.

Just before I returned to the university, I met up with an old school friend at his newly-opened restaurant. It had been his dream to open an omelet shop. I praised him for his success. He asked me what I wanted to do with my life. I shrugged and said, "I want to be a millionaire."

Preface

He told me to wait for a minute, as he had something for me. He returned with a copy of Napoleon Hill's book, *Think and Grow Rich*. He told me to read it and use it to help me achieve my goal. More than forty-five years later, I still have the book, although the pages are tattered and the binding is weak. This one book gave me the tenacity, direction, and fortitude to overcome all the challenges I faced as a single mother trying to navigate through life. This book kept me focused and determined to succeed.

Another book, *Kriya Yoga* by Kriyananda, added the dimension of soulful connection. Without a soulful grounding, all the success in the world is meaningless. This book set me on the path of soulful pursuit, where I have practiced, studied, written about, and taught karma yoga for more than thirty years. Along the way, I found a saying on a tea bag that changed my life. It said, *if you want to learn, read; if you want to know, write; and if you want to master, teach.* And so, for more than thirty years I have practiced, written about, and taught karma to thousands of students, and now I would like to share with you *how to work your karma so your life works for you.*

As I began to work my karma, my life took miraculous turns. After many years of raising my children and doing jobs I detested, I was finally in a place where I could take the plunge into the depths of my soul and discover how to prosper with a purpose.

Soon into my soulful travels, I met my husband. Together we have traveled the world. I have written books and produced health programs with international distribution and recognition. I did it by mastering my karma. I won't say this is easy, but once you learn how to work your karma, life becomes easier and more meaningful. I also became a self-made millionaire!

Not bad for a kid who grew up in a poor fishing village on an island off the coast of Maine!

Just remember that every obstacle in life is an opportunity to discover the secret meaning and purpose of life. When you discover this and learn how to work your karma, you begin to prosper with a purpose.

Without a purpose what does it all mean? They say when the student is ready the teacher appears. Are you ready to prosper with a purpose?

Namaste.

May you always travel the soulful path with health, happiness, and peace.

Doctor Lynn

Introduction

I asked myself:
Why is all this s*** happening to me? What did I do that was so bad that my life was a constant struggle? These are the questions I asked myself over and over as I struggled to understand what my life, and life in general, was all about.

My first revelation into these questions came to me when I was wanted by the FBI for questioning. My ex-husband and I were two confused young kids caught up in the hippie era of protesting the Vietnam war and the fight for civil rights. My ex-husband was a young guy in the military, and I was an activist with a naïve view of the world. We left the United States, snuck across the border into Canada, and became fugitives. My ex-husband was a deserter, and I was wanted for questioning by the FBI because they thought I was involved with a very radical underground movement planning to storm the U.S. border. Really, I was just a scared and confused young kid looking for acceptance and love.

We went to Toronto and began to work for the American Deserter's Committee. We lived in a commune and our job was to help other draft dodgers and deserters get across the border and get granted landed immigrant status. I discovered that running away from something was not going to fix either my problems or the larger problems of life. If you want to fix something, you need to fix it from the inside first. So, that meant retuning to the U.S. and actively making a difference in a peaceful manner.

I won't say this put me on the path to success, but it did begin to open my consciousness. It made me see that if you really wanted to change things, make a difference, and better your life it had to start by working on yourself. It was time to stop feeling like a victim and stop fighting the establishment. It was time to start working on my inner self and becoming the person I needed to be. This was the beginning of discovering my karma, and although it took many years and many trials and tribulations to discover how to master and use it to master my life, this was an invaluable lesson. You need to do the work from the inside first and then send it out into the world.

I have spent over forty years as a naturopathic doctor and yoga master practicing, writing about, and teaching holistic health and karma yoga. I have run hundreds of workshops, helped hundreds of students and clients, received international recognition as a writer and producer, as well as lectured at universities. The one question that I kept hearing was, "How did you know this was just the message I needed to hear?" I was just sharing what we all intuitively know; that life is full of obstacles. It's how we handle these obstacles that makes all the difference in our lives. Just get on the soulful path.

I have walked this soul-walking path, and it has made all the difference in my life. And now I will share with you the intricacies, secrets, and steps that will show you how to work your karma so your life works for you. In this way, you will discover how to prosper with a purpose.

Karma is about working the inner consciousness to expand your awareness of the dynamic power of energy. This is why we are here on Earth. Learning how to harness and direct the energy of your soul while mentally and physically navigating life will help you discover your purpose and the meaning of your life. The greatest drive we all have as human beings is to answer the questions: Who am I and why am I here?

This takes inner work, but we cannot just go within to find the answers. We also need help from the material world if we are to prosper with a purpose. The world is real, and as such it is here for us to learn, know, and master life. But we must be willing to do the work of discovery, and when we do that, the work gets easier. Once we learn how to direct our energy, we begin to achieve remarkable success. Karma means working on our own state of being in a selfless and meaningful way, and when we do that, we begin to master our lives. Health, happiness, and success can be ours, but we must work to achieve them. This is not an abdication of self, but a connection to the true nature of our being. It is an opportunity to discover our purpose and the meaning of our lives in a very practical and pragmatic way.

This book is a practical guide to help you uncover why you are here and what your life is all about. I will take you down the soul-walking path, where I will teach the true meaning of karma and how it works. You'll discover some things that have been blocking your progress. You will also find within this book your correction, or the main piece of karma, you are here to work on in this life.

If you have found yourself burnt out, frustrated, fearful, discouraged, and lonely while questioning, wondering, and pondering the purpose and meaning of your life, this guide is for you. By taking this soul walk, you will learn how to use your energy, body, mind, and soul to bring wealth, pleasure, harmony, and liberation into your life. That's what it means to live a prosperous life with a purpose.

Each chapter is organized to take you on a soulful journey of discovery. We start from the beginning; how did you get here?

Next, you'll begin to understand what karma is and how you can best use it to improve and enhance every aspect of your life. Then we'll move on to the discovery of what it means to live a prosperous life. And finally, you will discover the container that holds all of life's treasures. At the end, you can find a glossary of terms to refer to as you integrate these concepts into your life. I will show you how to open the container, take out the treasures, and then how to use them to prosper with a purpose.

It has been said that a good teacher shows you were to look, but not what to see. I hope to be that teacher for you.

Welcome to the journey!
Doctor Lynn

CHAPTER ONE

How Did We Get Here?

*"Traveler what do you seek here . . . since this
world is not your final resting place?"*
KRIYANANADA

So just how did we get here in this life, at this time, and in this place? According to karma, we reincarnated.

To fully understand karma, we need to begin with an understanding of reincarnation.

Whether you believe in reincarnation or not it is an interesting subject for most people. According to karma yoga and physics, we are simply a bundle of energy. And according to the laws of thermodynamics, energy is never lost, but simply changes form. Therefore, our energy field (body, mind, soul) is seen as a subtle form of motion, like a wave or a pulse that goes on and on.

To fully understand anything, we must understand it's opposite. So, if we can only know "on" by knowing "off," is it possible that we can only know we are alive by knowing we had once been dead?

If we are simply a bundle of energy, and we follow the laws of thermodynamics, we can conclude that our energy is never lost, it simply changes form. So, it would stand to reason that when we die, our energy just changes to a different form of energy, and that energy maintains the potential to return again to Earth and change its form again.

According to karma, the *"soul"* purpose of our Earth life is to find our way back to that perfect infinite source of energy. This involves working through our Earth karma. So, like an echo from the past we are called back to Earth to complete this mission. To do this, we break away from the infinite source of potential energy and take on the finiteness of human life.

The laws of karma state that when we transcend to the astral world (die), we are not weighed down by emotions and are free to make an accurate appraisal of our past deeds and misdeeds. We then decide what areas need improvement and what areas need to be atoned.

Karma teaches that when we leave this world, we go to the holdover place, which is not the final resting place. It is a place for reflection. Free of emotions and sensations, we process our desires in terms of what we wish to experience again, what we wish to experience for the first time, and what we wish to correct. Because we cannot accomplish this without human emotions, experiences, and sensations, we return to Earth to take on earthly form and begin again. After we have reached the decision, we find and choose a suitable body and parents that will best help us accomplish our mission.

Before the soul decides to be born, it will decide what karmic debt it intends to repay. It then selects the parents and life situation that will best help with this karma. Since physical incarnations are difficult, souls incarnate near, or with, some of their loved ones from previous lives. These loved ones are the ones that help to influence our evolution.

About six months into a woman's pregnancy, according to karma, the soul enters the fetus. When the right astrological time is near, the soul activates the birthing process so the soul can be born at the exact time for karmic obligation to begin.

On the spiritual plane, the karmic debts appear reasonably easy, but in the physical world we once again experience pain, cold, heat, grief, fear, and physical limitations. We may become so frustrated with the load of our karmic debt that we forget what we set out to do. Life then becomes a repeat of a former life with different props and players. However, if the new self does meet the challenges of life, the individual is on the road to enlightenment. Transcendence frees us from the hold of the ego and from the cycles of physical rebirth and death, as well as the wheel of karmic debt.

Reincarnation is not just an Eastern belief. The Kabbalah (Jewish mysticism) refers to reincarnation, as did the early Christian church. The Second Council of Constantinople denounced reincarnation in AD 553. At the time, it was thought that reincarnation afforded humans too much time to find ultimate salvation. They believed that humans would use this one life to enjoy the world rather than seek God and the truth. Fear was instilled to exercise control.

According to the laws of karma, humans reincarnate on Earth until they have regained their status as children of the spiritual universe.

The law of karma requires that our soulful desires find fulfillment. Non-soulful desires are the chains that bind us to the reincarnation wheel. Our present task is simply to make this chapter (life) of our evolution a happy and fulfilling journey. It is about releasing our soul from the bondage of karma so that we can find freedom, purity, and serenity.

Each of us left something undone in a previous lifetime, and this has caused us to return. The memories of what we did and did not do or say haunt our subconscious mind. Our subconscious mind is the seat of the soul, our intellectual layer of energy. It is the memory track of the spirit. Balancing the energy of the lower chakras and lifting our energy above the lower layers of our being allows us to tap into the intellectual self, and it is here that we have the opportunity to discover the soul's purpose.

The present is created in the past, or the memory. However, we must not be too frustrated if we do not accomplish all that we would like to in this lifetime. Simply let this chapter of your life be a reflection of a truthful, happy, and loving existence. Remember, this is only a chapter in the bigger book of soulful life. There is no time limit for completion of the book. And yet, in a sense, there is a hurry because if you wish to end your suffering and continual rebirth you must sincerely seek to transcend the lower humanly aspect of yourself.

When we uncover our karmic obligation, we are faced with a decision: to conquer our fears and guilt or allow them to overwhelm us so that nothing gets resolved. To awaken and grow we must be willing to become the witness and observer of our lives and learn to live from a place of compassion, faith, balance, serenity, peace, strength, and divinity. Not an easy task. That is why karma is called work. But the irony is that the harder you work the easier the work gets.

So, to discover our past lives or why we are here we begin by using karma yoga and meditation to bring about the calmness needed that allows us to slip into our subconscious intellectual self. Here we make notes to ourselves about what we are drawn to:

>What are your favorite foods?
>
>What part of the world, or culture, are you drawn to?
>
>What comes naturally to you?
>
>What is it in your life that flows?
>
>What is it in your life that is a recurrent problem?

Be on the lookout for people, places, and things that will give you clues.

Let me share with you one of my own experiences:

I grew up in an environment where it was not acceptable to indulge in Eastern thought, yoga, or mysticism. Being poor, it was all about making money and survival. Puritan New England called for conformity. To not risk being ostracized and to make a living, I went into business and hated every minute. In my private world, I studied yoga and Eastern thought. I experimented with unusual diets, herbs, and aromatherapy.

One day, I had a revelation. In a meditation, I saw myself as a young woman running along the edge of a forest. I was carrying a basket of herbs that I was trying to hide. I knew that I was hiding because I did not want to be persecuted for practicing my craft, which was herbal healing, thought at the time to be witchcraft. I hid from my enemies and then denied my craft so as to spare my life. My face was covered with misery and pain. I emerged from the meditation and realized that I had been denying my craft in this lifetime by trying to conform and get acceptance, when in fact I was destroying my life with my unhappiness. It was at this point that I gave up my other life and began to pay attention to the stories of my past. I sold my house, went back to school, studied naturopathy, and began my true journey. You see, we carry forward and relive the things that are out of alignment with our true selves until we discover and create change. Above all else we must be true to ourselves.

Reincarnation will not provide you with a straight and clear path. You will soon discover that from here to there is never a straight line. There will be many twists and turns, as well as many detours. There will be low valleys and high mountain tops, as well as many ravines. How low you go, or how high you climb, will depend upon your moral compass. Let it be your guide.

When life takes you on a detour, don't resent it, fear it, or avoid it. Be on the lookout for opportunities, adventures, and chances to learn and grow. You never know what you will find. Trust in yourself, follow your moral compass, and watch out for time gates. These are happenstance opportunities that seem to appear from nowhere and yet they are everywhere, waiting for you to discover them and then have the courage to walk through the gate. But remember, as long as karma is pushing you towards the gate, you are not on the path. Soul walking is the path of freedom. It means to consciously choose.

You must first discover your primary piece of karma and then neutralize it so that you can walk the path, not because of karma, but because you have discovered a sense of the true nature of your journey, which is to walk on Earth free from all encumbrances; body, mind, and soul.

Pay attention and make note of the things you are drawn to, the things that come naturally to you, and what appear to be random opportunities. Look out for the time gates.

CHAPTER TWO

What Does it All Mean?

Striving to find meaning in life is the most powerful force driving humans and causing them to ask: Why am I here, what does this mean, and where am I going? We sometimes refer to this as searching to discover our purpose. When you have a sense of purpose, your brain chemistry begins to change. These biochemical changes affect everything from your ability to meet challenges, to establishing wellbeing, and even to controlling your perception of difficulty and pain.

A sense of purpose is very powerful. We all want to know how and where to find it. Neuroscientists tell us that uncertainty creates a negative impact on the brain. If we are confronted with a situation that is contrary to our values, things can get uncertain, and this uncertainty leads to the perception of a threat. A perceived threat, of course, creates stress. However, our brains are hardwired to avoid threat and/or move toward reward. That is why we are the happiest when we have a purpose and can find meaning in our lives. Knowing your purpose therefore creates a positive impact on the body, the mind, and the soul. But it is not enough just to find your purpose. You must then understand how to develop your purpose if you are to prosper and be successful. This requires following a prescribed set of steps known as **SOUL WALKING**.

These prescribed set of steps have been followed by alchemists, Jews, Buddhist, Hindus, Muslims, and Christians, as well as all cultures that quest to know, because everyone wants to discover the key to immortality and salvation.

Karma yoga teaches that humans come to Earth with impurities needing correction. We are here on Earth to learn how to cleanse and purify our karma so that we might finally transcend the birth and death cycle. This requires work.

But none of this can happen without knowledge of the most powerful force that exists. Next to the human soul, it is the most precious thing on Earth. Pay attention and you will discover this most valuable gift. It is everywhere, and at the same time difficult to attain. However, it is available to anyone who does the work to discover it. It is both loved and despised. It has the power to change the direction of humanity. Pay attention and at the right time this secret will be revealed.

In the following pages you will discover **your primary karma,** or what you are here to correct. Then, you must freely choose to work on it. Without working on your correction, you cannot prosper. You will also discover your purpose and glimpse into the meaning of life. Everything in your life will improve, including your health, your love life, and your career. You'll find courage and gain power leading you toward success. Ultimately, you will discover what it means to be in harmony and at peace with the world.

But first you will need to know what to look for and what to do with it when you find it. The following pages will show you the guidepost and the rules of the road while helping you develop a plan that, if followed, will bring you prosperity. This is not a simple "think positive" method. It is set of tools to help you uncover the meaning and purpose of your life. It takes work, but that work will bring you prosperity. To prosper means to have good fortune. What could be more fortuitous than to live a prosperous life?

Do you want to know why you are here? Would you like to discover your purpose? Would you like to master your life? Are you ready to prosper, succeed, and find wealth? Read on. Pay attention as the answers to these questions reveal themselves. These are not secrets; only things that have not been revealed. Once revealed you will *know, time gates will open,* and then you will begin to prosper.

Welcome to Karma Yoga!

CHAPTER THREE

Time Gates

Time gates are passageways, or spaces we step into at a particular time that change the direction of our life. Time gates exist everywhere without regard for time. They are simply space providing the means for change. When we refer to change, we refer to time and not space. However, all points in space are relative to one another, and therefore a time gate cannot exist in empty space. It must be linked to a specific event, and events happen as a result of time.

Wherever you are in the world, you will be faced with time gates. These gates are constantly opening and closing. When we step through a time gate, we either consciously or unconsciously set off a stream of time-space events that can have a powerful influence on our lives. In an instant our lives can change. An artist is discovered, a lover is found, or a leader is toppled.

From the outside, it appears that a person's life has changed dramatically for better or for worse, when in fact one has simply stepped through a time gate and the space one occupies has changed. Whether it is prosperous or not depends upon awareness and a number of circumstances. What might appear to be a stroke of luck might turn out to be a burden.

There are creative and prosperous time gates, and then there are destructive and disastrous time gates. It is our level of perception and the depth of our wisdom that determines which gates we step through and which we avoid. Our karma will draw us to certain gates and bind us to others. The gate to prosperity may open before us, but because of our karmic blindness, we might walk right by it.

Being aware and open to opportunity allows you to discover time gates. You cannot be in a hurry to find them, but you must know what you are looking to find and then stay open to all the possibilities.

Being stuck in negativity and living at lower layers of your being will blind you from the prosperous time gates and bind you to the destructive gates. Free up your energy, lighten your load, and keep your eyes open for opportunity. Learn to work on your karma and be aware. The prosper time gates will open for you when the time is right, but you must be aware and know when and how to step through them. Just remember…

Don't Confuse the Map for the Territory

Here is an example of a time gate. I was living in Maine and wanted to move to LA but had no idea how I was going to do this. I kept feeling this tug to move west. One day, when I was working with a real estate client, I mentioned I wanted to move to LA. Later that day she called me and told me that her son had been offered a job in LA but was going to turn it down. The company was looking for people to move and would pay all the moving costs. She gave me the contact information. I contacted the company, was hired, moved to LA, and it completely changed my life.

Be on the lookout for time gates!

CHAPTER FOUR

Karma Particles

Now, before we get into a deeper understanding of karma, keep this in mind. When we reincarnate, karma particles come into our lives in percentages, and these percentages have a great influence on the nature of our lives.

1. The smallest percentage of karma relates to the **length of your life.** No matter what you do, negative or positive, this karma determines the length of your life. The percentage is 5 percent. This is an interesting concept, as we can see that the length of our life is not nearly as important as the nature of our life.
2. **Name and fame** equal 6 percent. Each is an equal 3 percent, so your name and the level of notoriety are 6 percent of your reason for being in this incarnation.
3. The karma that determines your **individuality** equals 8 percent, and the karma that determines your family and family origin is another 8 percent, for a total of 16 percent.
4. The karma of **knowledge, happiness, and awareness** each equal 12 percent, for a total of 36 percent. Remember, negative karma can block happiness (12 percent of

your being), just as it can hinder knowledge and the awareness to see things as they truly are.
5. **Belief and conduct** each make up 9 ½ percent of your karma for a total of 19 percent.
6. The karma of **joy** equals 18 percent. The greatest amount of negative karma goes into prohibiting the expression of joy.

What this means is that your karma is divided into percentages, and these percentages rule different areas of your life. **We cannot change our individuality or our family of origin,** but **we can change the other 84 percent: name and fame, knowledge, happiness and awareness, beliefs and conduct, and the expression of joy.** We have chosen to return to a particular family as a particular individual for the completion of our lessons. Using these percentages, we can see ways to improve our lives.

It wasn't until I found karma that I began to appreciate my individuality. There is no one on Earth like me living my unique life. Even with all of life's ups and downs, you are here to discover the amazement of the individual soul.

CHAPTER FIVE

What is Karma?

Speak of karma and everyone raises an eyebrow and turns to listen. That is because karma is so misunderstood. Everyone wants to know **why** am I here, **what** does this mean, and **where** am I going? Striving to find meaning in life for humans is our most powerful driving force. To question life is the fuel of ingenuity.

This book will reveal your karma and then teach you ways to change it and soften it so that you will draw prosperity into your life.

This is not a positive thinking self-help book, but a method of discovery that will lead you towards a life of prosperity. You'll learn how to correct the repetitive mistakes you have been making, and with this you will change the way you view life. It takes work—that's karma!

Sometimes in life it is better to define something by what it is not. That is probably the best way to understand karma. In our Western world, we use the pop culture definition of karma as actions that are good or bad. We use phrases like, "What goes around comes around," or "It must be my karma."

Good and bad implies judgment. Karma is not about judgment. Judgment is really a very subjective impression. Good and bad signifies punishment, or retribution if a deed is not morally correct. But morally correct is also a subjective impression and often based upon cultural norms. What might be morally acceptable in one culture may be different in another. For example, in some cultures if you steal you get your hand cut off. Other cultures find this morally unacceptable. So, karma is not the impressions, but rather the result of certain actions. Whether you get caught or not, punished or not, a thief is a thief and the impressions of stealing get embedded into the subconscious, or the soul. Tell lies and you become a liar whether you are found out or not. You carry this energy and it has an effect upon your life. Karma, therefore, is not about punishment or rewards, but simply the energy of cause and effect.

Essentially, the laws of karma state that every action, thought, word, or deed produces a physical or mental effect. It also produces an invisible intention, or inclination. This proclivity is stored in your soul (the memory track of your spirit). Everything that we do, say, or think affects us on all planes: body, mind, and soul.

Because the invisible effects of our actions are stored in our souls, they endure beyond our Earth life, maintaining the potential to be energized in future lives. According to karma, the soul chooses the nature of its Earthly experience based on the desire to present itself with the potential to work through these invisible impressions, or pieces of karma.

Karma is present energy that, under certain conditions, changes from invisible to visible form. We look upon these manifestations as either rewarding or punishing when in fact they are simply results of past actions and attitudes. **Basically, life becomes what life does.**

All creation is the result of energy. The process of creation is change. So, remember everything that happens is the result of past action, whether it happened a minute ago or lifetimes ago. Karma is a result of the past.

If a person comes into this life able to sing, play an instrument, draw a picture without any effort, or easily undertakes any task, according to the doctrine of karma, he or she probably began the endeavor in a previous life. Therefore, the doctrine of karma states that nothing in life comes instantaneously. Everything is the result of a long learning process.

When we think about universal justice, we might ask the questions: Why me? Why was I born poor when others were born rich, or why are some born with physical and mental hardships while others easily move through the world? Why, when a plane crashes, does someone live while others die? Why is an innocent person murdered and the perpetrator gets away unpunished? Where is there justice in this? Karma teaches us that there is no such thing as universal justice, and that is why we need laws, or guideposts.

The law of karma simply states that all events are the result of a cause that becomes an effect and are ruled by how our karmic percentages help us do our karmic work. In life there are no rewards or punishments. Life is simply cause and effect. We are here to learn this valuable lesson: **Life becomes what life does; observe it and understand it.**

Before we are born, we choose the circumstances in which we have the greatest opportunity to discover the nature of our Earthly mission; what we are here to learn. To learn, we must seek knowledge and then turn that knowledge into wisdom. Be aware that karma is the way of action, and every action (cause) has its effect. The universe is a perfect accounting system.

Everything gets balanced. Nothing goes unnoticed. So be mindful and choose wisely.

There is also a special karma you create in this lifetime that will annihilate karma from the past, as well as karma in this lifetime and in future lifetimes. Just remember that karma is not retribution. It is an emotional and mental impetus from the past, and that past could be one minute ago or many lifetimes ago. Be on the lookout for this special karma. It will help you to prosper. What is it? Look for opportunities to develop virtues and remove vices and you will discover it.

Because life is simply cause and effect, our energy causes our thoughts to materialize. Our thoughts then take on emotional qualities. How we manifest these thoughts create the form and function of our lives. Remember that energy is carried forward from our past lives and is brought into this life not as a punishment or reward, but as a means of presenting us with the quickest way to learn our karmic lesson. **The question then becomes: what is your lesson?**

Before we can discover the lessons, we have come here to learn, we must reincarnate. According to karma, in the last forty-eight minutes of your last life, you had desires. These desires must then be realized again through your next life.

As we depart this Earth, we leave behind our bodies and our Earthly senses. The soul cannot experience Earthly desires without the help of the body and the senses, so it chooses to return. For example: desires may be of a craving or addictive nature, which means that the addiction, drama, and negativity will intensify in the next lifetime.

There are three forces of karma enticing us to return for another lifetime experience:

1. Our deepest wish is to be free of all karma, and therefore we return to annihilate all karma.
2. Our desire to taste (experience) the things we tasted in a previous life. These are the cravings and desires of the flesh.
3. The desire to taste (experience) things we never tasted before.

According to karma, we leave this world with unfinished business. We go to the holdover place which is somewhat like heaven. It is not the final resting place, but simply a place to reflect. When the time is right, we make the decision to return to another life in an attempt to fulfill our mission and remove our karma.

The soul does not possess human senses, and thus must return to Earth in human form to experience the desires of this lifetime. We choose the nature of our birth and the structure of our lives as the most expedient way to teach us our karmic lesson. This does not mean we accomplish our mission in this lifetime or the next. We keep trying until we get it right. A lifetime, according to karma, is simply a blink of time in the universe. So, according to karma, we are eternal and infinite, like the energy of the universe, and therefore have many lifetimes to gather the wisdom we seek. Choose wisely and you will discover wealth, pleasure, harmony, and liberation; the freedom that comes when you are at peace.

According to the doctrines of karma, we choose our mothers and fathers and the circumstances of our lives. Our mission is simply to discover the truth and to choose the best circumstances that will present us with the greatest opportunity to discover this truth. Whether we do so or not is up to us. Karma does not dictate. It is simply cause and effect, which can be changed through our awareness of how to use this energy.

There are eight types of karma we encounter in our lifetime. The first is **attitudinal** karma. All karmic events are processed through the attitudes we carry. Our attitudes determine the outcome of our experiences and our lives.

The second is **event** karma. Certain events happen in the course of our lives that create change. Marriages, birth of children, divorce, death of loved one, change in job, and other Earthly events that help to shape our lives.

The third is **time gates**. We have all had experiences or known someone whose life has suddenly taken a drastic change. Like the starving young actor who suddenly gets a break and his whole life changes. It is said this person has passed through a time gate. Time gates are everywhere, and due to our attitudes, we can often walk right by an opportunity.

The fourth is **reciprocity.** We reap what we sow (cause and effect), and so what we give out into the world comes back to us.

The fifth is **generating.** We are constantly generating karma by our actions. It will either manifest in this lifetime or the next.

The sixth is **supportive** karma. This is the action we perform that supports karmic change. An example would be counseling or practicing yoga.

The seventh is **counteractive** karma, or doing things that are counter to the karma we are trying to work out. This is when we know we should be acting in one way, but act in another and thus create self-sabotaging actions.

The eighth is **destructive** karma. This of course is action that we take that deepens our karma or adds destructive consequences to our lives. A life of crime or drug addiction would be destructive examples.

To overcome a piece of karma, or to implement a lasting change, we need to apply a simple formula. Karma yoga teaches that it takes 120 days to overcome a piece of karma. This is called a trine pattern. A trine is what astrology refers to as an aspect, or the distance between two planets. A trine is the distance of 120 degrees. A trine symbolizes good luck. Modern science tells us that new red blood cells in our bodies regenerate about every 120 days. So, most likely it would take about 120 days to lock into your cellular memory something that you would like to change. So, focus on a change you want to make and stay focused on it for 120 days to make a change. Not easy—takes work—that's karma!

Our emotions are energy impressions embedded into the protein structure of our cells. Our body is constantly building up and breaking down these protein structures. Any emotional energy stored in your cells will be regenerated into new cells. The question then becomes: how do we best implant new energy memory into the cells? Karma teaches us that the best way to learn a lesson and implement change is **through awareness, meditation, contemplation, reflection, and vicarious learning.** By observing and consciously becoming aware of the karma we are attempting to change, we can and will learn the lesson. Karma tells us that if the lesson has been truly learned (change has been made), a space opens, and we then have a greater opportunity to manifest our free will. We become the masters of our destiny, and this leads to prosperity. When we learn how to work our karma, our life begins to work for us.

Recap: Karma is simply energy that moves—there is a cause and effect to all movement in the universe. According to karma, we have chosen to reincarnate choosing our parents, the place and time of our birth, and the environment that will give us the greatest opportunity to work through our karma.

We are ruled by our karmic percentages. We can change 84 percent of them, but we cannot change our individuality or our family of origin.

Pay attention to the things you can change and the things you cannot change. Know the difference and you will prosper.

CHAPTER SIX

Make Punja not Papa

Before we get into identifying your primary karma and the work you are here to do, we need to understand "Punja" and "Papa."

"Punja" and "Papa" are Sanskrit terms used to describe the law of karma, which is cause and effect.

Punja means to gain merits by doing good deeds. It's the accumulation of our positive thoughts, actions, and intentions. Sometimes referred to as "good" karma, it can lead to positive outcomes in the future such as health, happiness, and success.

Papa refers to the accumulation of negative actions, thoughts, and intentions. These negative actions, sometimes called "bad" karma, can lead to negative outcomes in the future, such as illness, suffering, and failure.

Working your karma means to cultivate punja and reduce papa. We can do this in a number of ways, such as practicing karma yoga and learning to master our ego.

When we master the power of the ego and begin to harness and redirect its energy, we remove papa or the obstacles blocking our pathway, and then we enhance punja or the merits that lead us to a prosperous and successful life. By enhancing merits, the consciousness expands, and with this expansion of potential energy comes a greater ability to deal with the concerns of everyday life. If we are to prosper, we need to be able to deal with the chaos of life in a balanced and calm manner.

But as well as removing "papa," we also need to make punya, which means merits or good deeds earned through our action in this life and our past lives. When we see people who are wealthy and successful, the Buddhists and the Hindus would call this pin that was earned from a past life. We in the Western world might call it luck. Karma yoga calls it the "good" karma you have earned from your past lives, as well as the merits you are earning in this life.

The result of creating punja is not necessarily in the form of money. It might appear as talent, integrity, virtue, value, beauty, status, worthiness, assets, honor, or goodness. We all carry these within us, just waiting for us to find them. Maybe we will discover them in this life, or maybe not until the next.

If we want to create punya we must exhaust papa; demerits or bad karma. Remember that karma attaches itself to our actions, our thoughts, and our speech. So, if you want to create punya, you must exhaust papa. The result of the creation of papa might appear as dishonesty, disturbance, evil, worthlessness, demerit, fault, or weakness.

The three basic methods of developing merit or punya are: **giving without expecting a return, living a virtuous life, and spreading good will.** These fall in line with the ten ways to make merits. They are:

1. Giving
2. Observing virtue
3. Concentrating
4. Focusing

5. Honoring others
6. Being of service
7. Dedication
8. Being happy for others' good fortune
9. Listening to and practicing virtuous teaching
10. Instructing others in being virtuous.

Consciously focus on doing good deeds, and the result will be prosperity.

CHAPTER SEVEN

We are Here to Prosper

We are here in this life to learn our lesson, make our corrections, and prosper. Whether we do this or not depends upon how we use our energy. Karma yoga teaches us how to embrace our Earthly soulful work so we can make the corrections that lead to a prosperous life.

A less familiar branch of yoga called *Padmini Vidya* teaches us how to become prosperous so that we can make our lives and the world a better place. *Padmini Vidya* is the science of the subtle forces used to attract wealth, and thus success. But wealth is not just about the accumulation of money and material goods. **It is about the active and willful control of the energy of consciousness toward one's benefit.** This is the greatest source of wealth. When we combine our karmic work with the practice of *Padmini Vidya* we prosper.

The Energy of Prosperity

Everything in life is a byproduct of energy. Therefore, if we wish to be successful in life, we must learn how to harness the energy of prosperity. Shakti in Hinduism is believed to be the cosmic energy that moves through the entire universe creating ability, strength, power, potential, and capacity. Shakti energy is the force that both maintains the universe and makes it disintegrate. Shakti is known as the spouse of Shiva, the Hindu God responsible for creation, upkeep, and the destruction of the world. Together they enter into a dance of creation and destruction. This energy is believed to lie dormant within each of us at the base of our spine, waiting to be awoken and lifted to our highest level of consciousness where we realize we are both the creative and destructive energy of our lives.

Padmini Vidya is the yoga of prosperity. "Padmini" means lady of the lotus and "Vidya" means the science of yoga. The lady of the lotus refers to Lakshmi, the goddess of wealth and purity.

Lakshmi is personified as the shakti energy and is also the wife of Vishnu, one of the principal deities of Hinduism. Vishnu protects all humans and restores order to the world. He is found in all aspects of creation, as well as destruction and regeneration. Together they enter into the dance that either creates or destroys. Used wisely, their energy will protect and regenerate. This dance has the potential to create prosperity and exists within each of us.

Lakshmi, the goddess energy of prosperity, is a powerful force. Her name means "aim" or "goal." She has four arms, which signify her power to grant the four goals, or directions, towards a successful and prosperous life: wealth (artha), worldly pleasure (kama sutra), harmony by adhering to a good moral and ethical code (dharma), and soulful liberation (moksha).

The aim of the four goals is to direct your highest potential into creating a prosperous and fulfilling life.

Prosperity is seen as good and necessary for a healthy and successful society, as well as for the individual. Surprisingly, only a small fraction of yogis denounces the material world.

That's because yoga is really a very practical scientific method for living a balanced life. It does not denounce anything, but simply calls upon us to consciously inspect how we conduct our actions through karma; the law of cause and effect. We must remember that every action in life creates a reaction, just as a mirror reflects an image. If we wish to prosper, we must pay attention to how our thoughts, words, and deeds both create and destroy.

Contrary to what some people may believe, the practice of yoga is not about living in a cave in an impoverished, austere manner. The practice of yoga fully acknowledges the realities of living in a material world. It encourages us to incorporate the four important goals of soulful growth, meaningful work, pleasure, and wealth into living a fulfilling and meaningful life. Yoga encourages us to prosper while consciously paying attention to how we use our energy. Life is a dance of creation and destruction.

Lakshmi reminds us that affluence should be respected because, in reality, affluence is a forceful stream of energy that has great power. It can create or destroy depending upon how we use it.

In the tradition of *Padmini Vidya*, wealth is not the accumulation of material things. Wealth is the ability to manipulate the energy of consciousness so as to bring about prosperity. Material things come and go, but once achieved, the consciousness of prosperity is eternal. It becomes our frame of reference and our way of looking and acting within the world.

The material world, on the other hand, is a constant flow of changing energy. Youth changes to old age and day to night, but the consciousness of prosperity, once found and fully understood, is eternal. You carry it with you forever.

Although many people have the determination to create wealth, their attitudes in doing so can greatly influence the outcome. The accumulation of wealth takes more than positive thinking. It is a mindset that seeks to create. But we should remember that inert symbols of affluence are not wealth. Wealth is the byproduct of the energy of prosperity. As you think, speak, and act, so you become.

Padmini Vidya reminds us that creation and destruction are powerful forces. But we should be forewarned; many sacred texts mention Alakshimi, the evil sister of Lakshmi. With disregard for order, disrespect of nature, and poor hygiene, she will bestow poverty and misfortune upon your house. Pay attention to what you do with your energy.

If you want to bring prosperity into your life, let the energy of prosperity flow out towards others. Apply the Golden Rule of prosperity: **do not take without giving back.** Those who look for ways to help others and ways to contribute to the betterment of life, without expecting anything in return, are sure to prosper. They have found a need and are fulfilling it. This brings us wealth in many forms.

The goddess Lakshmi tells us that prosperity has far more to offer us than a beautiful home and a large bank account. Death won't let you take any of these things with you. But abundance of potential energy brought into existence through conscious thought will bring you wealth. You are the source of your wealth. **Whatever you have, increase it. Instead of saying it could be less, say it could be more.** Say, "I would like to have this," but do it from a place of consciousness and contentment. Be content with what you have and then reach out for more. Lakshmi gives wealth and success to those who ask with sincerity and are willing to do the work. **The work**

involves developing conscious awareness of how to use the dynamics of potential energy in complete harmony with the soul's path. This requires the ability to work your karma. When you combine the infinite force of the soul with the finite source of the material world to create good, anything and everything is possible. This is the pathway to prosperity.

Remember this: the most abundant thing in the universe is energy. Use it wisely. The punja, or merits we accumulate as we travel through life, are with us from lifetime to lifetime. They define us and are by far our most valuable assets. Money can't buy you happiness, but prosperity can!

> "Although you may gather a million gold coins upon your death you cannot take with you even one copper penny."
>
> (CHINESE PROVERB)

CHAPTER EIGHT

The Four Aims Leading to Prosperity

Lakshmi has four hands which represent the four main directions, aims, or goals in life that will bring us prosperity. She reminds us that we must work our karma, respect the energy of creation and destruction, and remain steadfast in our aims if we wish to be successful and prosper.

The First Direction or Aim in Life is the Accumulation of Wealth

Don't confuse wealth for money. Money in and of itself is valueless. It is only what we can purchase in exchange for money that gives it value. **Wealth is abundant potential energy.**

The Kama Sutra, a Hindu Sanskrit text, makes it clear that health, love, and pleasure, as well as music, art, and education can only flourish in a prosperous society. Poverty, therefore, is not a virtue. It can actually be an obstacle, especially when it comes to morals and ethics. It can be somewhat difficult to be moral and ethical when you are starving and struggling to survive.

Material wealth allows for the refinement of society, and this refinement allows us the opportunity to partake of pleasures and to be kinder and more generous.

Wealth is not just about the accumulation of money or material goods, although both have the power to make the world a better place. Wealth comes in many forms such as good health, love, happiness, and rewarding work. Many people get lost in the illusion of material wealth and confuse the Earthly symbols of wealth for success. Success is measured by the degree of your happiness and not the size of your bank account.

In this world, no one would argue that it is better to be rich than poor. Wealthy people have greater access to the necessities and the luxuries of life. Wealth affords more options and choices. But just remember this—it is not wealth that destroys. It is greed.

Problems arise when wealth is used to control other people and to abuse society. In a world such as ours, with so much wealth, no person should ever go without or be abused. So, if you want to prosper, find a way to make the world a better place and you will become a wealthy person.

Just remember the difference between wealth and material possessions. Wealth can mean having beauty, love, and good health, and these can never be replaced with gold, money, or other material possessions. Your true wealth comes from within. It is the source of your abundant energy, and this energy has the power to create. Draw from it, create, and you will prosper. Once found, this cosmic energy can never be depleted. Just remember that energy is never lost, it simply changes form. As long as the universe exists there will be infinite opportunity to tap into this abundant energy and with it, create prosperity. Money may come and go, or slip past your outstretched hand, but if you use your abundant energy wisely you will always create **wealth and with this you prosper.**

The Second Aim in Life is Pleasure

As human beings we are wired for **pleasure.** The human drive is not simply to survive; it wants to thrive, and to thrive we seek pleasure. We are programmed to strive for survival and longevity, and an essential part of this is the drive towards pleasure. What would the world be like if we could not enjoy the pleasures of life?

Some interpretations of yoga appear to denounce pleasure. It is thought to distract us from our karmic work. But pleasure is as essential to life as air and water. It is the engine that drives us to create and thrive. The key is to never take pleasure to excess. Always be moderate and balanced. *Seek balance in all things and in all things find balance.*

Your primitive brain, also known as the limbic system, is located in the temporal lobe at the base of your skull. The limbic system is made up of multiple parts, such as the hippocampus, which is your memory center. The basic drive for survival, sex, food, and sleep all take place in the limbic system. The part that is responsible for basic pleasures and pain is the amygdala. The amygdala is our fear-based alarm system. Once fear and pain set in, we immediately seek to replace them with pleasure.

The amygdala is the part of the limbic system which is involved with emotions and other reactions to stimuli. It contains many neurotransmitters, with the central nucleus of the amygdala most strongly modulated by dopamine. In other words, it senses fear or threat and then reacts quickly to remove the fear or threat and replace it with our desire to experience pleasure rather than pain.

Serotonin, as well as dopamine, is a neurochemical that also effects our level of pain and pleasure. Both dopamine and serotonin need to be in sync if we are to be balanced. Where dopamine drives us towards pleasure, serotonin keeps us content, relaxed, and satisfied. And although it can take pleasure to extremes, dopamine is necessary for our survival and our ability to thrive. Therefore, the drive to seek pleasure is essential to both the survival and the thriving of humankind.

Neuroscientists point to the nucleus accumbens as the pleasure center of the brain. All addictive behaviors from drug abuse to gambling cause a powerful surge of dopamine in the nucleus accumbens. Dopamine, the neurotransmitter that gives us a sense of pleasure, is the neurotransmitter made in the brain that acts as a chemical messenger between neurons. It is released when your brain is expecting a reward. It creates a cycle of motivation, reward, and reinforcement. The right amount of dopamine brings us balanced pleasure and is ideal for learning, planning, and productivity. But a flood of dopamine can create a feeling of euphoria, which can lead to addiction and mental health issues.

So, we can see that on a purely biochemical basis humans are wired to avoid pain and seek pleasure. The problem arises when our chemistry gets out of balance due to illness, poor health, or addiction and we fall into the rapid urge to seek a false sense of pleasure to avoid pain. The pleasure eventually fades, and we find ourselves back into a state of pain, craving pleasure, and then the cycle repeats itself.

The pleasure a drug addict gets from the fix is short-lived and soon is replaced with the pain of seeking the next fix.

As well as being necessary for your survival, pleasure has many levels and layers. Just remember it can also be destructive if we allow pleasure to control our desires to the point of addiction. But pleasure at the deeper layers of our being instills beauty, and when pleasure and beauty come together, we truly understand the importance of enjoying the real pleasures of life. In harmony with life, pleasures are never destructive, but always uplifting. Understanding this, you will begin to prosper.

It's not pleasure that destroys the good. It is deceit and greed. We sometimes greedily deceive ourselves into believing we need more. That is why yoga teaches us to enjoy life, but always in moderation and never to excess. It is our desire for excess that tips pleasure into pain. Just ask an addict how much pleasure there is in seeking the next fix.

The Katha Upanishad, from an ancient Hindu text, teaches us to overcome pain by understanding it. We cannot bargain with life, but we can come to understand that all of life is a process that involves experiencing both pleasure and pain. It reminds us to not take our life for granted. Enjoy the pleasure found in the moments. Our dreams and our desires are part of life. So, enjoy the pleasures of life, for life is short. But we must be reminded to keep everything in balance, or else we tip the scale from pleasure to pain. Stay unattached to things. We are here on Earth to understand our existence and to see how we can use all the experiences of life to broaden our knowledge. You cannot bargain with life or death, but you can make peace with these two opposing forces through good character, soulful aims, restraint, dutifulness, knowledge, and the choices you consciously make.

Karma teaches that a wise person will always choose to do what is good over sheer pleasure. This can be interpreted a number of ways. One way is that a wise person will choose what is good over the pleasure of comfort, or a wise person will choose to seek pleasure through effort and depth over laziness and superficiality.

The greatest pleasure comes from the greatest depth of our soul. When we truly experience something with full involvement by tapping into its essence, we discover the true nature of pleasure. We sometimes call this "being in the flow" or "in the moment." Whether it is eating chocolate, sipping a great wine, buying a gift, making love, or spending tons of money, it's not the pleasure that should be avoided, but the greedy, deceitful, self-serving nature of the ego. The ego always wants and thinks it deserves more! So, to tame the ego, practice moderation in all things and in all things be moderate.

Pleasure has both a physical and an emotional aspect. Pleasure is comprised of five layers; it is sensual, loving, has a purpose, is creative, and exercises free will. All these layers are important to humans. They bring us pleasure but can equally bring us pain if we are not careful in how we think, speak, and act. Just remember, all things in moderation.

Sensually connecting with someone you intimately love for the purpose of creating is the closest two souls can get to willful pleasure. The more aware you are of the nature of pleasure, the more likely you are to discover it and use it wisely.

The Third Aim in Life is Harmony

Our third aim should be to move in harmony with life. This requires a code of ethics and morals that act as beacons telling us how to behave. In yoga we would call these the "yamas" and "niyamas." These are akin to the Ten Commandments, as well as the Ten Virtues of Buddhism. In fact, there is no religion or spiritual belief without some form of moral and ethical codes. These are the foundation stones without which nothing lasting can be built. They remind us to practice nonviolence, truthfulness, non-stealing, sensual control, non-greed, and to observe purity (cleanliness), contentment, austerity (simplicity), to study the scriptures, and to have faith.

These basic suggestions give us a guide for creating harmony rather than disharmony. Disharmony creates discord, and when we are in discord with the world prosperity is diminished.

To use an analogy: when it comes to music, harmony builds upon an already existing melody. In its more literal sense, a melody is a combination of pitch and rhythm. Rhythm is defined as the pulse or beat of an activity. Plato made the observation that rhythm is "an order of movement." So, for harmony to exist there must be an order to the movement of energy.

Whatever other elements a given piece of music may have, rhythm is the one indispensable element of all music. Rhythm can exist without melody, as in the drumbeats of so-called primitive music, but melody cannot exist without rhythm. In music that has both harmony and melody, the rhythmic structure cannot be separated. So, if we take an analogy from music; to move in harmony with life we must have a rhythm or an order of movement that causes it to be harmonious.

It is so easy to get caught up in the dramas, problems, and stresses of life and to believe them to be the final reality. All that happens in your life is simply an opportunity to discover and correct your karma. When you begin to understand this, you will discover how to bring rhythm and melody together in every situation to create harmony.

The irony of life is that for all our outward striving and drama, in the end, the sum total always adds up to zero. We take none of the dramas, problems, and stressors with us when we depart this world. What we do take is the karma of our experiences. How we use these experiences defines our next reincarnation. If life hands you a difficult problem and you face it with compassion and understanding, you create harmony and not discord. It is not the problem you take with you when you depart this world, but the virtue of compassion, and this will assist you in this life and all the other lives to come.

By cultivating harmony, we develop compassion and understanding with all our relationships on Earth. We move from being separate and bound by the ego to merging past the barriers that keep us apart and at odds. When we develop impartiality towards all things of the world, we become one force of energy that endures under all circumstances. However, impartiality does not mean to be indifferent. It means to be undisturbed by the ebb and flow of life. This is how we create harmony.

According to the philosophy of karma yoga, the whole material universe consists of five everlasting, enduring substances. It is through these five substances and their relationship to each other that the whole world unfolds and evolves.

These five enduring substances are **space, motion, rest, matter, and soul.** Space is the container of everything; motion is required for change to occur, and rest is necessary for matter to accumulate. Matter exists as a finite number of points of energy that come together by resting in space. The soul is the unifying energy or essence that gives birth to potential. Therefore, we and everything in the universe exist as matter occupying space with the potential to create. Create harmony and you will prosper.

For the most part, relationships provide us with an opportunity to create harmony or disharmony.

In all relationships, but more specifically in love relationships, we are constantly moving between coming together and moving apart, holding on and letting go, yielding and taking the lead. Most people find this dance so difficult. Often, they find themselves deadlocked into opposing positions where they create disharmony. Communication breaks down and we take flight or fight. The dance becomes one of creation or destruction.

If you have ever experienced an inharmonious relationship either in your work, your family, your love life, or any aspect of your life, you know the feeling of anguish. It disrupts not only one part of your life but disrupts all the other parts. Disharmony within a family causes disharmony at work, at play, and to your health.

So how do we maintain a harmonious balance with life? How do we stay on the sharp edge of existence without being too close or too distant; without the risk of losing ourselves? We want freedom and yet we strive for stability and commitment. We want love and yet we get angry. How can we get close to life, be familiar and comfortable, and at the same time return with a sense of passion and love? **We must learn to walk the "middle way."**

The middle way means to not become identified with anything: love or hate, happiness or depression, attachment or detachment. Instead, you simply come back to the present moment, putting aside all attachments to any position. Just remember that right now one thing may be important, but circumstances will happen and tomorrow it may lose its significance.

Harmony requires commitment, understanding, patience, forgiveness, a lot of hard work, compromise, balance, flexibility, strength, and respect. It means to put aside our attachment to being right, or even being wrong, and come back to the present moment and do what it takes to remove discord. Then, just like in music, arrange the notes so that what we experience is melodic harmony. We now move gracefully in rhythm with life, and this creates prosperity. Most everyone likes to be around harmonious people.

Remember, the whole material universe consists of five everlasting and imperishable substances: space, motion, rest, matter, and soul. What's important is how matter relates to other matter within the space it occupies. All of life is equal, but different, and that is what makes life so interesting. Harmonize with life and the obstacles that block success will be removed and you will prosper.

The Fourth Aim is Liberation or Staying on the Soulful Path

The journey of life is not about your body or your mind, but about your soul. But without the health of your body and your mind, the journey is useless. We spend so much time fretting over the configuration of the body and either denying it or giving it pleasure that we lose sight of its purpose. We thrash about in our minds, bashing our lives with self-loathing, complaints, and fear, forgetting why we took on this body, this mind, and this life. We are here to understand life and thus to discover liberation. Don't confuse liberation with having the freedom to do whatever you choose. Liberation means reaching a level of peace with life just as it is; it means becoming the observer of life free of disturbance and judgment. With liberation comes wisdom.

Change is the only absolute, so why is it so difficult for us to accept it? We seek out the permanent aspect of everything because it makes us feel safe, content, and connected. We try to control the impermanent aspects of life because the unknown causes us to feel anxious and fearful. But impermanence is exactly what we need if we are to find the ultimate prize of life, and that is liberation; the freedom to accept things and to let them come and go without attachment.

There is a proverb that goes, "The more things change, the more they stay the same." This refers to the ever-changing element of nature held fast by the never-changing essence of life.

Everything in nature is constantly changing, right down to the molecules and cells of your body. But the underlying essence of life stays the same. Love, hatred, war, peace, feast, and famine—life will always present us with the basic challenges of existence. It is our approach to these things that constantly changes. Since the beginning of time, humans have waged war and conflict. How we approach it and what we call it has constantly changed.

We will always need food and shelter. We will always seek love and acceptance, and we will always feel fear and anxiety. This is a part of human nature. But if we can develop the ability to pause and catch a breath at the wonders of life, we will realize that everything is simply an opportunity. Become the observer of life and you will discover liberation.

You are here to learn, know, and master life, and with this comes wisdom. Without all the experiences of life, wisdom can never be found. One thing I know for sure about **wisdom** is that it **doesn't come easy,** and experiences don't come without living a full life. To discover liberation is to embrace all of life without attachment, but never be indifferent. This leads to wisdom.

Wisdom is sometimes defined as knowledge. But plenty of people have knowledge with little common sense or judgment. **Wisdom is far more than knowledge;** however, it does require knowledge and experience. Wisdom is the ability to learn, know, and master your life. Wisdom is in knowing the right path to walk. Integrity is walking it. This is the great challenge of life.

Science defines our wisdom as **crystalized intelligence**. This simply means that as we age and gather experience, our minds hold a vast amount of knowledge which we can draw upon. Young brains may be quicker, but older brains can more readily reach for a solution to a problem or make a decision because of experience and crystalized intelligence. Would we call this wisdom? Perhaps we could, but wisdom is so much more than experience and knowledge crystalized into accessible information. It's not how much information you store, but how you use it that keeps you on the soulful path. Wisdom is more than intelligence. Wisdom is in knowing that everything constantly changes, so don't get attached to anything. It is also the realization that time has wings; it flies, so don't waste it. Just remember—*you never step into the same river twice*. **Choose wisely, walk softly, and stay on the path.**

Along the soulful path there will be many divergences and zigs and zags. From here to there is never a straight line. There will be times when you wander so far off the path you will get lost. You may get caught up in the maya of life and lose touch with what is real. But if you stay on the soulful path, you will learn how to use the world to realize your highest potential without letting the world use you. This is how you master life and prosper. Karma yoga teaches us that everything is simply cause and effect. What you think, say, and do is what you become. Aim each day to bring wealth, pleasure, harmony, and liberation to yourself and to the world. When you aim for these four directions while working your karma, you will discover the container that holds the treasures of life, and in this you will prosper. But first you must understand how to work your karma.

CHAPTER NINE

What is Your Karma?

Before we can prosper in life, we must learn how to identify and address the karmic energy that continually manifests in our lives. These we call the four great passions. To be passionate is not "bad." Passion just needs to be directed in ways that bring us prosperity.

You may have a piece of karma that calls upon you to live out a difficult situation, such as an unhappy marriage. This may be the lesson for learning unselfishness, sharing, respect, and truth. If you had learned the lessons prior to the marriage, the experience of a difficult marriage would no longer be needed. A space then opens in our lives, and instead of the karmic lesson of difficulty, you experience a marriage of joy and love.

According to karma, our true purpose in life is to return to a state of balance, love, happiness, and abundance while removing our negative karma. A change in attitude is usually what brings about a change in karma. However, be careful with attitude because what may work in one moment may not in another. Our desires are what keeps us in the ever-repeating pattern of karma. While there is value in the repetition, it is of a higher value to transcend the rebirth cycle of karma and find our true self, which exists in a state of balance, harmony, love, happiness, and peace.

If you choose to break the pattern of your karma, you will free your energy to explore the rest of the universe, and through your wisdom you will realize that you now can do as you choose rather than being compelled by karma. This is because you now know that there is something beyond the body-mind, and that is your essence also known as the soul. Your soul is free to create and thus bring about change.

The root of all karma is seeded in the four great passions. One of these passions is more intense in your life than the others; but they all appear at one time or another. The four great passions which are the major causes of all of life's problems are:

Deceit

Greed

Anger

Pride

These states, which lack honesty, tolerance, unselfishness, and humility, are the triggering mechanisms for all karma. They also include a lack of sincerity, fairness, joy, admiration, detachment, and courage. These give rise to prejudice, sorrow, disloyalty, fear, disgust, and cruel joking, which will activate karma and get us into trouble.

Deceit to most of us means to lie or not tell the truth. But deceit is also the ability to live in ignorance and denial. Blaming others for the nature of our present and past existence is a form of deceit. We lack the awareness to face ourselves with honesty. In each of us is a small voice that always speaks the truth. Because we do not wish to hear it, we create diversions. When the voice comes up we suppress it, because facing the negativity within ourselves fills us with fear. When we understand the laws of karma, we realize that the inner voice is simply a cause that brings an effect that is not a retribution or message of our badness. In an objective state, we realize that it is simply the lesson we have come to learn.

Here's an example of deceit: In one of my workshops, a woman named Julie discovered her main karma to be deceit. At first, she was very upset, believing she was a good, caring, and honest person. As we worked on her karma, she began to see that she had always been a caregiver to others. She had done it because she wanted others to love her and so she would give so much of herself to others with little in return. She resented the selfishness of others. Now she could see that she had been deceiving herself into believing that she would be loved and considered a good person if she gave. Her resentment was the result (effect) of the cause to give in order to receive a feeling of self-worth. She discovered that she was deceiving herself by looking to others for approval.

Greed is a passion from which we recoil. No one likes to think of themselves as being greedy, and yet each of us on some level has been consumed by greed. When we think of greed we usually think of avarice, or excessive hoarding of money and material things. Greed is fixation upon objects of sensory pleasure and gratification. For example: alcohol, food, or sex. Greed causes us to commit violence against others and ourselves. In the practice of yoga, if we push ourselves beyond our limit while doing a particular asana (pose), it is said we practice greed. Because we desire to keep up with the teacher, or go beyond the other students, we risk injuring ourselves. When injuries happen, we contract and must stop our practice and heal our injuries. We therefore stop the flow of evolution and growth. Greed imprisons our time, emotions, and energy. It has nothing to do with the possession of things and money. It's really about a feeling of inadequacy, and thus not wanting others to have more than we have. We feel a lack of empowerment, and therefore greedily hold onto what we believe to be the most important source of our self-definition.

Unselfishness and giving for the sake of giving transcends greed. We can often appear to be acting for others when in fact because we are not free of self-interest our deeds are simply pretexts for receiving gratitude. To transcend greed, we need to give without any expectation.

Anger is probably a passion with which we can all identify. It is something we have all experienced. Although no one likes to be an angry person, it is somewhat easier to admit this passion than the other three passions. Perhaps that is because anger is seen as a worthy passion if it is used to right an injustice. However, it is very difficult to practice the right amount of anger at the right time for the right reason.

Another student, Cherie, discovered that her karma was anger. She had a feeling of abandonment that had left her anxious and depressed. She was lonely and had been searching to find her soul mate. She just wanted to connect and give, but because she held onto her anger, she idealized life and felt frustrated and imprisoned in her loneliness.

Cherie is an insightful woman and very open to looking at her inner self. She strives to improve in a soulful sense. So, she began to look at herself as a person who needed to let go of her hurt and anger before the door could open to bring love and joy into her life. I watched her aura change and her energy lift from this point on. She wore a new hairstyle, took a couple of trips, and is now more relaxed and at peace with herself. She has lifted the dark cloud of her karma and I have no doubt that she soon will find her soul mate.

Pride is a passion I know well, for it is my correction, or karma. It is also the correction of another young lady named Karen who has attended my workshops. Pride is insecurity and fear turned outward in an act of defiance. For me it was all about survival. I was so ashamed of my humble beginnings that I set about to prove to the world that I did not need anybody. I was strong, independent, and braver than most. Through my foolish pride, I drove others away. I found myself to be a lonely and self-absorbed individual crying out for love and devotion. Because of my pride, life presented me with many humbling experiences. From these, my own inner work allowed me to see my pride and its self-destructive nature. Through my work, which has come to be my karma, I have learned to let go of shame and step past the maya (the illusion). Pride is a false sense of self-acceptance.

Karen found her pride in her arrogant, defiant, nonconformist self. Pride helped her to keep others from getting close. This is how she was able to survive. If she gave off an air of not caring so no one would know she was crying inside. Her pride was her ego boldly keeping the world at bay. The realization of this passion allowed her to see her pride surface within her life's experience and to correct it. I am most proud of Karen for all her hard work. She has grown into a most beautiful young woman, whose courage and depth will take her far.

I would like to mention all the women who took my first karma workshop, because they are the bravest women I know. Each came with a mission, and that was to look deeper into her inner self so as to bring a greater sense of balance and understanding into her life. They came prepared to be open, honest, and sharing. They stood in support of each other. I humbly have learned so much from each of them. So, thank you to the following beautiful women: Ilene, Angie, Tracy, Arlene, Jodel,

Nicole, Greta, Trudy, Cheryl, Judy, Marlene, Joy, Debra, Holly, Beth, Thury, Kerrie, and Terry. In each of us we find the other, and so it is with people of depth and character. Souls always speak to souls. You just need to know how to listen.

Our work here on Earth is to transcend all four of the great passions, which are the root cause of all our so-called problems. All four play a part in our lives. One will be stronger than the others and will be our lesson to learn in this lifetime. As we lessen the intensity of a passion through awareness, it is said that our aura softens and we take on a new, softer coloration as we change. The practice of karma yoga is one way to soften the coloration. Karma teaches that with the proper work the coloration of your aura will improve about every twelve years, with major coloration changes happening between the ages of twenty-nine and a half to thirty-two, fifty to fifty-two and a half, or eighty-eight and a half to ninety-one. These cycles can begin one and a half years earlier and thus end one and a half years sooner.

The best advice that I can give for softening the coloration of your aura is to stay young at heart as you grow forward. Remain open and flexible to change. Don't let yourself get rigid and cynical. Instill self-discipline, which means manifesting certain actions and inhibiting other actions.

The soul only wishes to know its pure divine self. It is our human cravings and desires that bring about discontent and suffering. As long as we are caught up in the cycle of discontent, we can never find balance and peace. Cravings and desires cloud our awareness, and thus we become what in karma is known as the "ignorant unaware-self."

Desires and cravings lead to selfishness. Desiring satisfaction for the sensory self, we are driven by the ego, where we fall prey to the four great passions: **deceit, greed, anger, and pride**. The selfish egotistical self is never satisfied. We must learn to tame the ego without extinguishing it, for it is an important means of self-preservation. However, the problems arise when the "I" (ego) that sits above the "me" (soul) believes that its reality is the one and only final reality. As we say in karma, be careful not to fall into D-GAP.

Although the soul has an infinite ability for creativity, it only has three central activities: **thinking, speaking, doing**. These three activities create our karma, and all karma seeks expression through our thoughts, words, and deeds.

Remember, to lighten or soften your karma (aura), you need to manifest certain actions and inhibit others. The practice of yoga (physical) helps us to learn to become motionless and balanced without losing consciousness. This is how we annihilate karma; being balanced and serene while holding onto awareness. **This is known as our "witnessing consciousness;" the observing principle of life.**

Although we must all work these four passions, one is more intense in your life than the other three. To discover which one is your great passion to master, go to the next chapter and look up your correction using your birthdate. These are general but will give you an idea of what you need to work on to master your karma.

CHAPTER TEN

What is Your Karma?

In a state of balance, the soul sees its true nature, which is its infinite ability to change and thus create. Creation is the key to changing karma, but first we must become aware. The following is from the book *Kabbalistic Astrology Made Easy* by Rabbi Philip S. Berg, who has been so kind as to let me include this in the workshop. I have taken classes at the Kabbalah Center in Los Angeles and met many wonderful people there. I wish to thank everyone at the Kabbalah Center. Look up your birthday and then find your tikun, or karmic correction. Each correction emphasizes one of the four great passions: deceit. greed, anger, and pride. Use this as a barometer of your karmic work in this lifetime. Don't take it too literally. Read it and set it aside, and then return to read it again at a quiet moment.

If you were born between these two dates, <u>your correction is:</u>

Scorpio—May 20, 1901, to Dec. 7, 1902
Libra—Dec. 8, 1902, to June 25, 1904
Virgo—June 26, 1904, to Jan. 12, 1906
Leo—Jan. 13, 1906, to Aug. 1, 1907

Cancer—Aug. 2, 1907, to Feb. 17, 1909
Gemini—Feb. 18, 1909, to Sept. 6, 1910
Taurus—Sept. 7, 1910, to March 26, 1912
Aries—March 27, 1912, to Oct. 13, 1913
Pisces—Oct. 14, 1913, to May 1, 1915
Aquarius—May 2, 1915, to Dec. 7, 1916
Capricorn—Dec. 8, 1916, to June 7, 1918
Sagittarius—June 8, 1918, to Dec. 25, 1919
Scorpio—Dec. 26, 1919, to July 13, 1921
Libra—July 14, 1921, to Jan. 30, 1923
Virgo—Jan. 31, 1923, to Aug. 19, 1924
Leo—Aug. 20, 1924, to March 7, 1926
Cancer—March 8, 1926, to Sept. 24, 1927
Gemini—Sept. 25, 1927, to April 12, 1929
Taurus—April 13, 1929, to Oct. 31, 1930
Aries—Nov. 1, 1930, to May 19, 1932
Pisces—May 20, 1932, to Dec. 6, 1933
Aquarius—Dec. 7, 1933, to June 25, 1935
Capricorn—June 26, 1935, to Jan. 11, 1937
Sagittarius—Jan. 12, 1937, to July 31, 1938
Scorpio—Aug. 1, 1938, to Feb. 17, 1940
Libra—Feb. 18, 1940, to Sept. 5, 1941
Virgo—Sept. 6, 1941, to March 25, 1943
Leo—March 26, 1944, to Oct. 11, 1944
Cancer—Oct. 12, 1944, to May 1, 1946
Gemini—May 2, 1946, to Nov. 18, 1947
Taurus—Nov. 19, 1947, to June 6, 1949
Aries—June 7, 1949, to Dec. 24, 1950
Pisces—Dec. 25, 1950, to July 12, 1952
Aquarius—July 13, 1952, to Jan. 30, 1954
Capricorn—Jan. 31, 1954, to Aug. 19, 1955

Sagittarius—Aug. 20, 1955, to March 7, 1957
Scorpio—March 8, 1957, to Sept. 24, 1958
Libra—Sept. 25, 1958, to April 12, 1960
Virgo—April 13, 1960, to Oct. 30, 1961
Leo—Oct. 31, 1961, to May 19, 1963
Cancer—May 20, 1963, to Dec. 5, 1964
Gemini—Dec. 6, 1964, to June 24, 1966
Taurus—June 25, 1966, to Jan. 11, 1968
Aries—Jan. 12, 1968, to July 31, 1969
Pisces—Aug. 1, 1969, to Feb. 17, 1971
Aquarius—Feb. 18, 1971, to Sept. 5, 1972
Capricorn—Sept. 6, 1972, to March 25, 1974
Sagittarius—March 26, 1974, to Oct. 12, 1975
Scorpio—Oct. 13, 1975, to April 30, 1977
Libra—May 1, 1977, to Nov. 17, 1978
Virgo—Nov. 18, 1978, to June 5, 1980
Cancer—Dec. 25, 1981, to July 13, 1983
Gemini—July 14, 1983, to Jan. 29, 1985
Taurus—Jan. 30, 1985, to Aug. 18, 1986
Aries—Aug. 19, 1986, to March 6, 1988
Pisces—March 7, 1988, to Sept. 23, 1989
Aquarius—Sept. 24, 1989, to April 12, 1991
Capricorn—April 13, 1991, to Oct. 30, 1992
Sagittarius—Oct. 31, 1992, to May 19, 1994
Scorpio—May 20, 1994, to Dec. 6, 1995
Libra—Dec. 7, 1995, to June 24, 1997
Virgo—June 25, 1997, to Jan. 11, 1999
Leo—Jan. 12, 1999, to July 27, 2000
Cancer—July 28, 2000, to Feb. 13, 2002
Gemini—Feb. 14, 2002, to Sept. 4, 2003
Taurus—July 30, 2003, to Jan. 26, 2005

Aries—Jan. 27, 2005, to Aug. 19, 2007
Pisces—Aug. 20, 2007, to March 7, 2009
Aquarius—March 8, 2009, to Oct. 12, 2011
Capricorn—Oct. 13, 2011, to May 2, 2013
Sagittarius—May 3, 2013, to Dec. 6, 2015
Scorpio—Dec. 7, 2015, to July 13, 2017
Libra—July 14, 2017, to Jan 29, 2019
Taurus—an. 30, 2019, to Aug. 18, 2020
Pisces—Aug. 19, 2020, to March 6, 2022
Pisces—March 7, 2022, to Sept. 24, 2023

Find your birth date and your tikkun

or karmic correction, and then read your correction sign as follows to find your great passion.

The Tikkun in Aries—Deceit

The tikkun in Aries signifies that you have formerly had the behavior of a Libra. You have often been in the position of an arbitrator but have been unable to settle conflicts because you refused to make a decision. Taking a position was uncomfortable for you since it implied hurting someone. Therefore, you have tried to unite the incompatible, and therefore, you suffered the consequences rather than made a choice. You have learned to compromise and will take any path to avoid confusion since you did not make any choices.

One of the major problems is that you sought flattery and expected recognition. You acted with the intention of pleasing others rather than doing what would have pleased you. On the whole, you have been overly dependent on the opinion of others, and this lack of autonomy has often led you to be aggressive soon after your initial act of submission to the judgment of others.

The tikkun in Aries reveals an individual overly concerned with aesthetics; your entire life has been centered on beautiful things and personal comfort. To maintain this lifestyle, you readily accepted certain compromises and abused the strategy. Your hypersensitivity has caused you many problems and you have paid dearly for combining feelings with logic.

Today, first and foremost, you must find your own identity, not in the eyes of others, but in your own. You must seek autonomy and reinforce your self-confidence, since this will enable you to discover your own profound nature. If you stop avoiding confrontations and face each situation as it unfolds you will come to a higher consciousness. You must want freedom and have certainty without needing or wanting approval from others.

You will find the second part of your life easier to manage. In fact, by passing your tests, you will gain awareness of your own evolution and thus consolidate your personality. You could experience a genuine spiritual uplifting provided you share with others without expecting any recognition in return—true sharing, for the sake of sharing. You could combine Libra's half-hearted altruism with Aries's enterprising, but egotistical spirit and thus receive abundantly as a result of your "awakening," having learned to know yourself and marveling at the sight.

The Tikkun in Taurus—Anger

This is one of the most difficult corrections to make. In fact, those who have their tikkun in Taurus have had, in previous incarnations, the attitude of a Scorpio, the sign of self-destruction. Hence you could still have some residue of that sign's characteristics.

First, you have been the victim of blatant injustices; you

may have been robbed or dispossessed. As a result of these bad experiences, you feel angry and distrustful of others. Your behavior is often malicious due to these ancient fears, and you will go to any length to hold on to your possessions. You would rather destroy your own belongings than have them repossessed by others.

Despite this destructive tendency, your social behavior is friendly and spontaneous. Though still a rebel at heart, in this lifetime you are constrained by your anxiety. Your supernatural powers have not always been used in a positive way, but this time, these gifts will help you reach elevated levels of consciousness as long as they are used in the service of others and towards more constructive goals.

The tikkun in Taurus also reveals an individual whose attitude toward sex is relatively unbalanced. You are passionate with a large sexual appetite that has caused many upheavals in your life, traces of which still are to be found in your present life.

To avoid having to confront the difficult situations you experienced as a Scorpio, you must overcome your fears. To live better, you must adopt the attitude of a Taurus; namely, to appreciate the beauty and pleasures of life, all of which have been bestowed upon you by the Light. By opening up to the wonders of this world, you will discover a universe that is a paradise of sweetness, and this will enable you to transform your belligerence into serene and positive behavior. Your former inner torments will be appeased by your newfound tranquility. You will learn to enjoy life, a Taurus's specialty.

This new approach to the world will let you express your sensitivity and your emotions without the anxiety-induced fear of losing your possessions. If you succeed in breaking out of this Scorpion envelope, you could transform your insatiable need for immediate gratitude into a true gift of generosity and thus come near to total correction: Divine Love.

The Tikkun in Gemini—Greed

This correction is mainly a case of communication. You have had the disagreeable attitude of a spoiled child. Like a Sagittarius, you have been a bull in a china shop. Unorganized, you have adopted the habit of living from hand to mouth, letting your instincts guide you.

You never cared much for the people around you. Even when married, you behaved as though you were single. You lived an active life and did whatever you wanted to do because nothing else mattered. You had neither specific goals nor true projects. You were so preoccupied with satisfying your own immediate needs that this goal took over your entire life. Your thirst for knowledge and study has undoubtedly led you to discover new horizons, but in the end, you have remained a solitary prisoner of your egotistical desires. You have never committed yourself to a specific cause and have refused to concern yourself with others—constantly fleeing from the constraints you feel sharing creates. Uncommunicative, you have confined yourself to your small immediate pleasures and are therefore unable to benefit from what the "Light" wants to share with all of us. Despite your talent for languages and your remarkable knowledge of nature, you have not benefited from your gifts because you have not shared them. You hunger for freedom. Ignoring social constraints, you eagerly seek justice, but for yourself alone. You neither cooperated with your fellow beings nor gave them much credit.

Those who have their tikkun in Gemini must learn to turn to others. You must change your attitude and become humbler. Exercising diplomacy and tact will earn the respect of those around you.

Your curiosity will give you access to the surrounding world, this time through a different medium: the sharing of knowledge. You will have to communicate at all levels: work, family, and relationships. This is the key to freedom, which you did not find in your previous incarnations. This exchange of ideas will result in new concepts, which in turn will lead to a true metamorphosis from savage to being civilized.

Furthermore, you will have to plan and organize your objectives. By adopting certain rules of conduct for yourself, as well as for those around you, you will succeed in exceeding your own limits and accomplishing your mission; namely, that of sharing your inner riches and the knowledge accumulated in your incarnations.

The Tikkun in Cancer—Pride

This person carries enormous pride, a Capricornian attitude inherited from a previous incarnation. Totally preoccupied with your social climbing you have had many professional victories in your previous lives. Today you go in search of this lost recognition. Honor and reputation have been your main motivations, while respectability is your barometer. As any Capricorn worthy of the name, you have done everything in your power to achieve your goals and have worked hard to be acknowledged. Without hesitation, you have undertaken impossible goals, if only to gain the admiration of others. Your grand principles burdened your life, overwhelming you with excessive responsibilities that prevented you from thinking of others. Consumed by your social missions, you were oblivious to other people.

From previous incarnations, you have kept the seriousness and discipline necessary to accomplish whatever goals you set for yourself. You appointed yourself as judge, and consequently condemned the mistakes committed by others. However, though you presented yourself as a guardian of the highest moral order, your deeds failed to show any mercy. As a result, you have not created many friendships and have often been considered a shameless opportunist. This comes from your previous lifetimes and has cut you off from the pleasures of life, compelling you to adopt a secluded existence in your secret universe.

The tikkun in Cancer forces you to give. Having known no sharing, either in your victories or in your reputation, you now will be obliged to abandon all your illusions. The key to your happiness resides in building a truly warm and loving home that is a new surrounding where you will learn what real satisfaction means. You will be filled with wonder, with the simplicity and spontaneity of a child; a sensation completely new to you. You will learn adaptability and experience fantasy, both of which you previously excluded from consideration.

By opening up to your family, you will discover a different world; giving up some of your pride will let you pay more attention to others. However, the most difficult renunciation is abandoning the established conventions and frames of reference to which you have anchored yourself for so long. This will be your way of becoming more spiritual, "dropping your guard" in order to give and receive. The key is generosity in both affection and deeds. By breaking your antisocial behavior, you will escape from your ancestral impediments and discover devotion, the ultimate satisfaction.

The Tikkun in Leo—Deceit

The person with a tikkun in Leo is an individual quite apart. Once an Aquarian, in your previous incarnation you were considered to be important and unique. You have a tremendous inner power, topped up by a fierce ambition. Nevertheless, you never have been a model for discipline. On the contrary, you seek originality at any cost and are a rule breaker. Due to this attitude, you have been deemed superficial and have not been taken seriously.

All the same, keeping yourself apart has actually strengthened you. Although you were confronted with many doubts, you overcame them. You have been very dependent on others, would give anything to be surrounded by people, and relationships have meant the world to you. You often have had the feeling of being abandoned, of not receiving in return what you have given. You have even tolerated abuse in order to be surrounded by people. Having allowed your friendships to dominate you, you never reached the evolution you would otherwise have had.

Such opportunities will present themselves again in your present incarnation, provided you learn to exploit your inner strength. You have been severely scarred by your lack of discipline, which constantly prevented you from concentrating on real goals. You already have an acute sense of justice and equality, and your energy has been utilized now and again for defending noble causes. You preferred, however, to deal with masses of people rather than the individual. You have always seen yourself in the future, forgetting the present.

The tikkun in Leo will help you abandon your personal desire for originality and opt for the development of humanity. You must pursue your path within yourself and not in the eyes of others; find your own road and resist following the crowd. You have, in fact, more than one key from your previous incarnation to use in this one.

First, you have to seek a true disinterested love. For that purpose, the path to be followed has almost been set for you: defending a noble cause, but only on the condition that it serves humanity as a whole. You will have the opportunity to take the reins, provided you do it for a spiritual reason; that is, sharing your inner strength with the world and using your creativity to reveal new human resources which, in turn, will help you accomplish your mission. Your success could be brilliant, opening up unknown horizons. Your future achievements become the barometer of your personal merit.

The Tikkun in Virgo—Greed

The person who has his or her *Tikkun* in Virgo has a very confused worldview. Like the Piscean, you have been absorbed by your dreams and fantasies and have paid dearly for your melodramatic inclinations. You were nourished by tragic stories because you totally lacked discernment in your previous incarnation. You succumbed to self-pity and were heavily dependent on others throughout your previous existence.

Confronted with numerous obstacles, you often failed to react energetically. Moreover, your excessive feebleness led you to seek refuge in drugs and alcohol. Your oversensitivity to the pain of others prevented you from relieving that pain. Notwithstanding, you had a lot of talent and could have become a famous musician or painter. Your intuition allowed you to act for others in order to help them. Unfortunately, you were not free of self-interest and your deeds were a pretext to receive gratitude.

To break loose from such a correction, you must approach this world differently. First of all, if you overcome your hypersensitivity, you will gain a more realistic and less melodramatic view of a situation. Your sentimentality has already nullified you at least once. If during this incarnation you do not get rid of it, this weakness will bring you face to face with this same obstacle once again. Essentially, you must stop your fretful and whining attitude and clear your life of this overwhelming mawkishness. You must learn to speak your mind for your own benefit from a tremendous if not unique opportunity: to meet in this life all the people who ill-treated you in your previous incarnations. This would be your chance to settle accounts; namely, forgive and firmly overcome your personal rancor. Preserving relationships at any cost and always compromising have not proven to be the right solution.

Pondering will be your new tool for tackling problems, while self-discipline and determination will help you keep your feet on the ground. Your new motto will be "here and now." If you succeed in establishing a more concrete set of values with which to detach yourself from emotions and gain independence from those around you, you will attain your ideal: to help the world.

Reason, rather than emotion, will help you seize the opportunities to put your dreams into practice. If you stick with your desires long enough to fulfill them, you will know love and inner peace. Later in life, you will control your judgment and combine striving for perfection with your exceptional intuition.

The Tikkun in Libra—Pride

In your previous incarnation, you were noted for your outstanding self-confidence. Like Aries, your high self-esteem obviously caused you a few disappointments. In fact, preoccupied with yourself, you wasted all your energy, and as a result had to undergo an almost constant state of agitation. Although you did work, you never built anything solid. This being the case, you were induced to overreact and assume aggressive attitudes. Your egocentricity limited your vision and you often had to grapple with problems in a narrow-minded fashion.

Frightfully egotistical, your limited circle of friends restricted your possibility to share, explaining your jealous, sometimes even hateful response to those around you. Throughout your previous incarnation, this attitude brought about a profound sense of frustration, which in your present life has provoked this inexplicable need to hide, which you translate into aggressiveness.

Your antisocial behavior has put pressure on your relationships, making you go through emotional breakdowns, an unhappy marriage, or disastrous associations. Your selfishness has pushed you to abandon partners for others you felt more appropriately met your needs. You have never known durable relationships.

The tikkun in Libra will teach you to sacrifice in its noblest sense. It will arouse in you a disposition to disinterested devotion, provided you want to free yourself from frustration. Teamwork also will help you regain certain equilibrium.

Moreover, you will have to learn sharing in its simplest expression: listen to the ideas put forward by others, ponder what has been said, and open up to the opinions of others. Thus, due to your connections, you will grow softer, capable of mastering your anger and above all your susceptibility. If you understand that your real aim is the success of a group rather than your own, then and only then can you experience true happiness. Only through total unselfishness will you accomplish your mission and find inner peace.

Furthermore, you must endeavor to see things through; a test you never passed. The tikkun in Libra is one of the most difficult ones because it implies nullifying your own enormous pride in order to correct the errors from your previous lives. For this purpose, you will be granted a rare opportunity that will gain expression, mainly in your marriage. In truth, through your union you will understand real sharing, gaining strength from loving someone else. Being the driving force behind your partner will become the motivation to relinquish your narrow conception of "I" and think "we." You will likewise understand that the aim is less important than the road to achieving it, and this new perspective will reveal new horizons.

The Tikkun in Scorpio—Pride

To say that a tikkun in Scorpio is a blessing would be an exaggeration. Having a tikkun in Scorpio is no bargain. You have had in a previous life the behavior of a Taurus; namely, slow and heavy. Having kept this mental heaviness, your evolution will not be an easy one. Firmly attached to certain frames of reference, you are, generally speaking, stubborn. This attitude has blinded you so much that you are very reluctant to change.

Very susceptible to bodily pleasures, you have been a consummate hedonist. Overly impressed by your environment, you have been in love with beauty and nature. On the other hand, you have been very passionate, pursuing material rather than spiritual assets.

Your life has been routine and empty. Owing to your reluctance to get too involved for fear of losing something, you never experienced any special events. In truth, this correction is a painful one because you were oblivious to spiritual ends. Hemmed in by obstinacy, you did not listen to others and therefore did not learn from them.

In your present life, you have to confront genuine transformation. Fortunately, you have what it takes to see it through. First, you must loosen your worldview and reorganize your life. Breaking your habits should be your priority. Thus, you will become aware of the illusions that burdened your spirit and overshadowed reality. You could experience the most beautiful karmic metamorphosis provided you tackle your previous attachments.

You must start considering others differently, not in the light of strictly material criteria, but for their own value as human beings. You might discover an aptitude for psychology, your own way of opening up to this world.

As time goes on, you will also become more independent, or rather, autonomous in your actions. You will abandon the rigid rules that marked your life for more spontaneity, and thus really taste freedom of action. In this way, you will prove yourself to be worthy of respect and love. This task could prove to be a painful correction because it might cause many losses. Provided you want to accomplish this transformation, you will have to accept its price, however high it might be.

The Tikkun in Sagittarius—Deceit

Here we have to speak not of one personality, but two. The individual whose tikkun is in Sagittarius had in a previous incarnation the attitude of a Gemini; in other words, a duality of behavior. Having always considered all aspects of your life from two diametrically opposing standpoints, you lived a life of deep uncertainty.

Decision-making has been your major obstacle; you could not establish a course of action and stick to it. Had you known to focus on your targets beforehand you would not have had to go through such a reincarnation! One of your problems has been a lack of concentration. Early in your present life, you will have to confront this same situation.

Due to your behavior, you have been considered superficial, and therefore, neither taken seriously nor considered worthy. Your instability hindered you in attaining a professional standing. Your flightiness and lack of determination have handicapped your evolution.

To be accepted in a group, you danced to any tune. Lacking a personal opinion, you acted like a courtier, tempting the strong and holding the weak in contempt. In fact, you never had real desires and followed fashion out of fear. Due to your "chameleon" tendency, you were often called a hypocrite.

Today, the tikkun in Sagittarius will teach you to confront each aspect of your life. You will have to engage in true introspection in order to define your aims and accomplish them. Your responsibilities and obligations will enable you to impose your own opinions.

You could bridge this transformation through loyalty. In fact, you will be so eager for justice that you will make it a stepping stone to express your refusal to compromise. Integrity and sincerity will become the keywords in your evolution.

You will have the opportunity to learn, and your accumulated knowledge will be a springboard to develop your personality and thus attain a certain level of wisdom. However, only by sharing this wisdom will you attain universal truths.

You will have to turn your back on your superficial past and finally confront this world's reality. Authenticity will be at the heart of your dedication. You will find your own identity and, in the end, discover your true mission on Earth: sharing your wisdom and revealing the truth.

The Tikkun in Capricorn—Anger

The doubts and anguish inherited from a previous life impaired the person whose tikkun is in Capricorn. Having endured the influence of Cancer, you have to deal with being constantly anxious. Throughout your past life you incessantly sought security, so much so that you had to take refuge in idealizing life. In this way, you managed either to conceal your problems or eagerly accepted the direction of others, thus rejecting all kinds of responsibility.

Who are you today? Your family, particularly your parents, has become the scapegoat for all your weaknesses: a rerun of your previous incarnation. Having been profoundly marked by your father's image, you had to start your life with this handicap. Alternatively, you could have transferred this attitude towards society as a whole.

Having organized your life around and according to the rules and laws of society, you could have gone into politics or become a great patriot if only to have a reassuring frame of reference.

Being a conformist, you never opened up to the outside world. You lived the life of a hermit, buried in your own corner. You relied on the material world to find your hoped-for security.

You shunned true connections out of fear. Just as in the past, you refused to grow; you assumed an infantile behavior to avoid taking risks. Furthermore, owing to your taciturn and hypersensitive character, you were not sought after in society. Your inner confusion pushed you to beg for approval from others. Above all, due to your lack of self-confidence, you curtailed your own experiences.

Now this correction in Capricorn will teach you maturity. First, you will have to cut the umbilical cord with your family. This alone will make an important starting point provided you really intend to do things on your own.

Next, not only will you have to accept your responsibilities, but also look for new ones to dispel your anxieties. By planning your objectives, you will consolidate your personality and find in each of your achievements the confidence that so cruelly failed to appear in the past. In this way you will get to taste the pleasures of risk-taking; no more fear of daring. Besides, you will enjoy committing yourself without forethought.

The key will be to find a worthy cause and identify with it. Thus, you could draw upon the necessary strength to face up to obstacles and not seek refuge somewhere else.

If you succeed in controlling your overflowing emotion, you will have gained self-mastery and thus the readiness to meet your karmic mission.

The Tikkun in Aquarius—Pride

This individual is a true monarch returning to correct pride. Ever since your last incarnation, you dominated your subjects like a Leo, the king of the jungle. You lived in the limelight, lavished with attention. At the outset of your present incarnation, you will seek the admiration to which you were accustomed. You loved flashiness and luxury and will not find it easy to do without. As one used to ruling over your subjects, climbing down does not come naturally. Moreover, overcoming your pride will not be the obvious thing to do, since pride has been considerably reinforced during your previous incarnation.

Although a court surrounded you, you were a true individual. No one would have dared stick his or her nose into your business! You arrogantly exploited your incredible power to control others. Considering yourself the center of the universe was your way of expressing need for love and gratitude. You had to struggle to discern reality. Having lived in an artificial world, you had difficulties in finding a spiritual path.

The tikkun in Aquarius will make you face certain difficulties in your marriage, namely, accepting a partner, an equal, with whom to share everything. Nevertheless, this constitutes an excellent preliminary "drill" to overcome your inordinate pride. By serving others, you will slowly but surely abandon your old preoccupation with your own selfish desires. You will have to exchange your sacrosanct independence for a new concept of life; interdependence. If you realize that this world is not "me" versus all others, but that we are all equal and at the same level, you will shatter the most burdensome and paralyzing image on the road to evolution, namely egocentricity.

By giving up honors and glamour, you will succeed in creating an immense restriction and thus apprehend the duality of your correction; your personal life and your humanitarian mission. The tikkun in Aquarius is, in fact, that of the true missionary; you will attain the consciousness of a cosmic reality, and as a consequence, feel responsible for humanity as a whole.

Moreover, you could experience an exceptional, if not unique, adventure in the history of humankind, provided you manage the most difficult restrictions; silencing your ego, practicing humility and modesty, and living in simplicity. On this road, you will know true friendship and perhaps even universal fraternity.

Having inherited a Leonine power, you will discover the strength necessary to overcome the task and this time round, will utilize it for the benefit of all. You will have the opportunity to participate in all sorts of developments taking place in society, striving for the progress of civilization.

The Tikkun in Pisces—Deceit

The correction of this individual deals mainly with the conscious perception of another dimension. In fact, your chief limitation, having had the behavior of a Virgo leading to a tikkun in Pisces, resides in your inability to detach yourself from logic; you think and live in a Cartesian (relating to Descartes) world. Life shows that there are other parameters, however invisible and intangible, that determine your destiny.

In your previous incarnation, you always saw the tree without noticing the forest. You were absorbed in intricate rationalizations which, although right in the beginning, did not satisfy you after all because you always examined only one side of an image, namely the material one.

Nevertheless, this has not helped you reassure yourself. In truth, by demanding factual perfection, you made your task more difficult than it otherwise would have been. You aimed too high and lost your self-confidence. This is the root of your reticence to experience emotions.

Your concern for details not only has made you forget the initial goal, but also turned you into an irascible and fussy person. Having fallen into excessive organizing, you lost all trace of spontaneity. Very rigid in your way of thinking, you were unable to listen and learn from others. Your present evolution will cut through this phase.

Although you categorically rejected the imperfections of this world, you did not endeavor to mend it. To understand and master your own life, everything was compartmentalized and labeled according to strict rules. You forgot that existence does not conform to the Law of Descartes!

This behavior also has caused you difficulties and disagreements in your sexual life. Due to your unwillingness to get emotionally involved, afraid of not being able to control a relationship, you forbade yourself to give way to emotional outbursts of any kind. Having fragmented your past existence, today you have to complete the puzzle. But how do you do this?

First, you must understand that you cannot perceive the essence of truth through your five senses or through logic. You must understand that a metaphysical reality is at the origin of every physical manifestation. If you give up analyzing the effect, you will perceive the cause. This will enable you to erase the doubts that for so long have troubled you and to gain a clear image, which will enable you to reach a more spiritual level of consciousness.

Experiencing emotions will help you change your perception of others. As you judge them less, they will offer you more. This will ignite in you a love for your fellow beings and reinforce your compassion.

And for Everyone

In life you will have to act on two levels; living in the moment while looking into the future and acting in the present to serve your universal mission. The key is to have faith in the cause you are serving. You could live a true rebirth and benefit from a genuine revelation of your major goal on Earth, which is to attain universal consciousness. This means to discover the underlying essence of life. It is called infinite energy, and because of its infiniteness it always has the finite potential to be.

I would describe it as the infinite possibilities (effects) available for final causality.

But be cautioned: in life you will be deceived, lied to, used, and abused. You will experience anger, fear, sadness, loss, hatred, greed, and all the emotional states that are part of being a human being. You will experience each component of the D-GAP: deceit, greed, anger, and pride. Humanness involves experiencing all the aspects of what it means to take on human form. One day you will die, and at first those closest to you will be shocked and take a little time to grieve. But then they will move on because that is what humans do. They can be a selfish, self-centered breed. What you do with your human experiences determines how you are remembered and what lessons you have learned.

When someone deceives you and destroys trust remember this; **trust is the union of intelligence and integrity. Ignorance and deceit are its counter-opposite. Where is the center of intelligence and integrity? It is located in the third eye; the seat of the intellectual self also known as the soul. Here you know beyond knowing. Remove emotion and trust yourself.**

Remember, your tikkun (karmic correction) is general. It is not to be taken too literally, but simply as a general guide to your karmic correction. Keep your primary karma in mind as you go about your daily life. You will see it come up again and again. Go back to your tikkun and reread it from time to time.

CHAPTER ELEVEN

Now You Have Your D-GAP

Armed with your D-GAP, you are now ready to start **Soul Walking**. Don't carry your D-GAP too heavily. It is here to assist you and can be easily changed. However, it will take some work. That's karma, so now let's begin to soul walk down our Earthly path.

After class one day, a student asked me a question about what it meant to be spiritual person. Someone she knows calls herself a spiritual person. I am going to try and answer her question.

Spirituality is different than the body, the mind, and the soul, and yet spiritualty is all three of them working together. Spirituality is the force that moves energy and causes life to exist.

A person is not spiritual. A person is soulful. As humans, we are all walking the path of life because of the spiritual force of the universe. We call this prana, or the force that gives rise to all of life. We are here with a body, a mind, and a soul working to undo some piece of karma.

The body is the vehicle. The mind is the GPS. The soul is the part of you that circles your body and sits behind your mind. It is your essence. Sometimes you will get a hunch, a feeling, or perhaps a quiet moment when you sense something deeper than yourself. It's the soul unfolding your mission. The spirit initiates the process of discovery. The soul discovers it and then brings it to the body and the mind. Practicing karma yoga, we use the body, mind, and soul to discover, and hopefully master, our mission, which is to make punja and remove papa.

To answer my student's question, most likely anyone who says they are spiritual may in fact simply mean that they are soulfully walking the spiritual path one step at a time. They are not the spiritual force, but because of the spiritual force they are on the soulful path. You are a soul walking the spiritual path and not a spiritual being walking the soulful path. There is a difference. The soul is you. The spirit is the force.

When trying to walk along a certain path you must take your time. The path from here to there is never a straight line. Karma yoga teaches us that nothing comes instantaneously. Everything is a long learning process. So **be patient and kind. Both will serve you well.**

Everyone is **Soul Walking** whether they are conscious of it or not. We are all living out this life in our own individual way and yet are connected to the whole. Look for the moments of AHA! These will lead you toward discovering life's treasures and living a prosperous life. Pay attention to the guideposts and work on your karma. Don't worry about mastering anything. Just be open and aware. The gifts of prosperity are everywhere. Look for the time gates. When a positive one opens, step through it. Remember we are all here just trying to do the best we can possibly do. Respect everyone's **Soul Walk**, but most of all enjoy yours.

CHAPTER TWELVE

Maya—the Illusion (what is real?)

Perhaps you've heard it said that "life is an illusion." What does that mean?

To delve deeper into karma and our purpose for taking this Earthly walk, we need to understand maya.

Maya means illusion or boundaries and can be quite confusing. It does not mean that the world is not real. The world is made up of real experiences through which we might gain real knowledge into the nature of our "purusha": our real being known as soul.

According to the doctrines of Hinduism and Buddhism, maya refers to the illusion of reality that we exercise in our everyday lives. Maya is the veil of illusion that hides the true nature of the universe and keeps us trapped in the karmic cycle of suffering and rebirth. It is not the world that is the illusion; it is our interpretation of life's experiences that distorts reality.

The world we perceive through our senses is not the ultimate reality, but rather our subjective version of it. For example, to truly know a tree you must become the tree and know tree-ness; impossible, and yet we believe we know a tree when we see one.

We perceive the world through our own version of our experiences, believing this to be the final reality. This makes us feel separate from the rest of the universe, leading to a sense of ego attachment. By realizing that everything is interconnected and that our sense of the world is the illusion, and not an accurate reflection of the ultimate truth, we can gain a deeper understanding of the universe and ourselves.

As we move through life, we become defined by our experiences. As our knowledge of life develops, we are constantly trying to refine what defines us. Understanding the nature of the real purpose of life, we no longer need to live within boundaries and false perceptions of what we should be or what we think will make us happy. Removing the maya, we see the proverbial forest for the trees. We begin to realize that our experiences are like the different trees; however, they make up one forest. The details of our lives are less important than the overall picture, and yet it is through the details that we have a chance to discover the lessons and the meaning of life. Karma reminds us not to confuse the map for the territory!

We control how we interpret the world by the choices we make. But when presented with a choice, how do we make the right one? Look to your purusha; your soul.

Millionaires come and go. Beauty fades. Everything ages. What might be important today may mean nothing tomorrow. Understanding this, we realize that the maya, or the illusion, is in believing that life is about boundaries, bank accounts, and material possessions. It is not the material world that defines us, but rather it is how we use the material world to define and refine our sense of self-definition. We need the world and all of life's experiences to help us create who we are; a physical and mental being assisting the soul's evolution. We need the material world to help us understand, create, and evolve. Learn to use the world, but do not be used by it.

Maya—the Illusion (what is real?)

Nothing in life is permanent. Everything is subject to change. You cannot run away from anything or stop things from changing. That is because change is inevitable and the only constant in the universe. The illusion is in thinking we can stop things from changing.

Life will present you with problems to solve and decisions to make. Most people want to run from their problems and hate making decisions. Caught in the illusion of life, they commit violence, take a pill, drink, spend money, and try to hide. When this happens, we become like ostriches, sticking our heads in the sand while leaving ourselves open and exposed to misfortune.

Instead, get calm, withdraw from the illusion, and then reflect on what's best for all. Remember you are here as a body, mind, and soul to do the work (karma) so that the soul evolves. Resolve issues, choose wisely, and you will find that the journey of life becomes easier. Awareness, compassion, and understanding will be your guide.

The world is kind of like a factory full of raw materials. We use these materials to create our version of reality. As we pass through life, we are shaped by our experiences. As our knowledge of life expands, we refine it to coincide with our beliefs and attitudes. At some point, through the practice of karma we come to realize that everything in life is temporary. Money, name, fame, position, youth, and beauty all can fade away in a blink. We have all seen millionaires become paupers, authorities toppled, and famous beauties become old and wrinkled. Once we stop running after the material world, we no longer need money, beauty, or youth to make us happy. We realize that all that exists is temporary and that true lasting happiness is found when we connect with our purusha, our true self. Here, we experience pure joy simply found through the experience and not the material world. But we need the material world and all that exists within it to discover who we are and why we are here; we are *purusha on a mission to evolve.*

Purusha is described as the individual consciousness. According to yoga philosophy, each of us has a unique consciousness acquired through our unique experiences that is separate from the physical, or material, world. Purusha represents pure consciousness, awareness, and our soulful essence. It is our identity carrying the accumulated karma from our past lives. As we connect deeper to our essence, we have the opportunity to liberate ourselves from the maya, and thus experience true liberation. Nothing disturbs us as we learn to detach, let go, and let be without indifference. Always be alert and aware.

We might have an experience and it does not bring us lasting happiness. So, we repeat the experience again, only to find that, once again, it does not bring us everlasting happiness. That is because we are still living from the ego's point of view. The ego is the part of us that gets attached to emotions such as anger or hurt and then sets out to prove these feelings are justified. If we get angry with someone, we declare that they made us angry and place the blame on them. We separate ourselves from the anger in an attempt to preserve our pride.

With maya, we identify our body with the physical world. For example: in a yoga corpse pose we attempt to let go of the body and transcend our mind. It's an attempt to connect fully with the purusha. If when we get up from the pose someone tells us we are chubby, we immediately get offended and re-identify with our body, and yet we are not our body, nor our mind. We are purusha; pure energy that has taken on this body, this mind, and this life to discover our true essence.

Maya, the illusion, tricks us into believing what we perceive is real. The world will always try to trick us into believing that our perceived illusion will bring us joy and prosperity. And although we intellectually know this not to be true, it is not easy to step back and take an objective view. Just remember: the world is real; it is our perception of things that is the maya, or the illusion. See things for what they really are; opportunities to adjust and correct yourself, and in this you will begin to master your karma.

Everything in the world is real. It is here for your evolution. The maya or illusion is in believing that everything is ego-related and more important than the journey of your soul. Use the world, but do not be used by it. Remember that you are a steward of life, so use it wisely. To overcome maya, detach without indifference. Observe everything with an objective eye. Remove the emotional attachment and you will discover clarity. You will begin to understand why you are here and what you are here to learn. See every problem and decision as an opportunity to learn, know, and master your karma, and thus you master your life.

Life cannot be understood through intellectual interpretation. Life can only be understood through experiences. See the experiences for what they are: opportunities.

To compete in life requires a strong body and a steady mind, but to be successful requires something deeper; a sincere and intellectual understanding of maya.

CHAPTER THIRTEEN

The Four Blocks

The habits you form are a result of repeated actions you initiated over lifetimes of experience, be they wise or foolish. In yoga we call this "samskara," or the impressions that get inscribed into the mental groove of our being. These grooves are formed by repetitive thoughts, patterns, or habits that get deeper over time. If negative impressions get ingrained, the mental emotional *self* is unable to integrate with the other layers of *self*—the physical, energetic, higher wisdom, and ultimately bliss. To prosper we must be fully integrated at our highest level.

Once you establish a pattern, it takes conscious work to dissolve it, or in the case of a positive pattern, constant work to maintain it. It may take lifetimes to work this through. That is the nature of karma. We are on an evolutionary journey from lifetime to lifetime to resolve and transcend our negative karma (patterns) and establish ourselves in "maksha:" the freedom to simply be in a state of eternal bliss. It is by the force of karma that we are born again and again in an attempt to resolve and complete this journey.

According to karma, ignorance is the source of all suffering, and this suffering is the result of the four patterns of karma that obscure, or conceal, the truth. Once the truth is revealed, we have the ability to transcend our karma.

The first pattern is the karma that **blocks knowledge.** Our knowledge of the world comes about through the five senses. When knowledge is blocked one cannot see the subtle connection between things and events. It is like the person who is emotionally cruel to their partner and cannot understand why the partner is cold. It also means to be open to continually learning. A person who thinks they know it all blocks knowledge, and this blocks opportunities to succeed.

The second is the karma that **blocks feelings, such as joy and grief, pleasure and pain.** Simply put, this means that you cannot separate the opposing forces of nature. We cannot remove night from day. They both exist as a reflection of the other. Every experience in life can be seen as pleasurable or painful depending upon how we interpret things. A mosquito bites you and you feel the pain of the itch. You scratch the itch and feel the pleasure in scratching. The same bite brings both pain and pleasure.

We are here on Earth as human beings to experience all the feelings and emotions that are a part of human life. Therefore, do not block your feelings, but rather control them with balance, strength, flexibility, and peace.

The third is the **karma of vitality,** which supports our **longevity or life span.** The theory of karma states that the longer you live, the more experiences you have, the greater your knowledge, and so the wiser you may become. The length of your life is one thing, but the vitality (health) of your life is another. The vitality you have now is a direct result of the last life. **Be tremendously enthusiastic** about life now and it will affect this life as well as the next life. The karma affecting your next life is formed during the last forty-eight minutes of this incarnation.

The fourth karma is that which blocks **your willpower.** When this kind of karma is operating, it makes us incapable of doing even the simplest of things. Negative thoughts grow and become more negative, more emotional, and more dangerous. This develops into anxiety, fear, anger, and even hostility. Finally, it breaks out into self-destructive actions. When you lose the ability to harness your willpower many complications will arise in your life.

Master blocked knowledge, blocked feelings, blocked vitality (unhealthy lifestyle), and inability to unblock and harness your free will and you will have the tools to work through your karma. But remember it takes work—that's karma!

CHAPTER FOURTEEN

The Troublesome Four

If you hope to prosper, you must also master the Troublesome Four.

Life will present you with envy, jealousy, resentment, and revenge. These are the troublesome four. As humans, we cannot avoid the troublesome four. It will require discipline, strength, balance, and flexibility to master them.

Envy is a widespread feeling today. We think of it as being present only in the business world, but it also rears its ugly head along the soulful path. Secretly, individuals may wonder how far the other soul has gotten and whether he or she has already reached a higher level of being. This of course creates conflict, as an unhappy soul may wish to inflict misfortune onto others. This conflicts with the guidepost suggestion of doing no harm.

Envy means to feel inferior to others and to desire that which you have not earned. Just remember that the material world is not a representation of what a soul has earned or is valued or worth. Don't get confused by what appears to be material success. Many people are good at acquiring things but lack the ability to achieve. To achieve requires effort, courage, and skill, and with this comes realization and fulfillment. Envy no one and a calm sense of peace will soothe your soul. The opposite of envy is admiration. Admire others and then seek to become your own unique aspect of those qualities. Be content with what you have, take pleasure in your life, count your blessings, and then reach out for more as a happy soul. Everything you desire will be yours. You will have earned it.

Jealousy is a morbid emotion that looks for anything that will cause suffering. With jealousy, an individual feels threatened by the loss of control over another person or situation. It is a feeling of suspicion and mistrust. Jealousy corrodes and destroys everything it touches. Jealousy is really a feeling of being unlovable and in constant danger of losing. It is based in uncertainty and fear. The opposite of jealousy is trustworthiness. It means to trust in your own ability to rely upon yourself to feel loved, honored, and worthy. Trust always has the advantage, because trust seeks to create goodwill and not destroy. Replace jealousy with trust in yourself and give up trying to control others or other situations. Find your balance, your strength, and be flexible to the ever-changing nuances of life. Trust in yourself.

Love yourself by focusing on your wonderful qualities. Use your trustworthiness to make the world a better place and jealousy will be replaced with prosperity. Remember this: even love focused entirely on another human being cannot bring fulfillment in the long run. Focus on your self-worth and you will find the fulfillment you seek. Transcending jealousy, we find divine and eternal love. This frees us to rejoice in the pleasures of others without envy or jealousy, even while dealing with our own disappointments and problems.

Replace jealousy with self-trust and self-worthiness and the worth of your soul will shine through in all of life's ups and downs.

Resentment is a negative state where an individual blames everybody and everything but themself for the state of his or her life. This individual feels they are the hapless victim of a cruel fate. Life is seen as unfair and full of disappointments. Resentment results from expectation. We expect something, and when it doesn't turn out as expected we experience resentment. We then begin to see ourselves as hapless victims when in fact the responsibility for our destiny and happiness has to do with how we see things and not what another person does or does not do.

Expect and you will surely be let down. With expectations, happiness is falsely measured not by inner experience, but by outward appearances. In a positive state, one realizes that they are the architects of their own destiny, and that the human mind, and thus the soul, have unlimited possibilities. Realizing that limitations are self-imposed, the individual is able to lift the veil of illusion (maya) and master one's own fate. You can see the forest for the trees. Unreal and unfulfilled expectations are the foundation of resentment. We feel disappointed, sad, and even angry. Take responsibility for your expectations. Let each experience of your life come and go without attachment, but don't be indifferent, and you will avoid disappointment and thus experience the awareness and knowledge that brings the joy of pure happiness. You cannot change what happens, but you can change how you view it. Let go of resentment and focus on your potential energy and you will prosper.

Revenge is an act of wanting to conflict hurt or harm on someone for an injury or wrong suffered at their hands. You want to even the score by one upmanship. Retribution in the form of an eye for an eye and a tooth for a tooth is the focus of revenge.

The worst thing about revenge is that it gets inside your head and hijacks your focus. Once revenge occupies the space within your head, fighting it is like fighting yourself. Be careful with what you let occupy your mind; it will occupy you.

It has been said that "revenge is sweet." The problem with revenge is that it can falsely make us feel good and powerful. It stimulates an area of the brain called the dorsal striatum, which gets excited when we anticipate pleasure and reward. But studies have shown that the feeling of pleasure and reward is overshadowed by the focus on punishment. Punishment usurps our ability to focus on reward. Revenge does not make us feel better.

The desire to get revenge is a mighty powerful force. If you take that energy and redirect it towards improving your life, you get the greatest revenge of all; **you prosper.**

> "Revenge is never a straight line. It's a forest.
> It's easy to lose your way . . . to get lost . . .
> to forget where you came in."
>
> HATTORI HANZO (PLAYED BY SHINICHI CHIBA IN KILL BILL VOL.1)

To master the Troublesome Four requires balance, strength, and flexibility as well as the ability to be content and at peace with your life just as it is. Circumstances happen. You cannot un-happen them. Accept what happens. Learn from it and focus on using what you have learned to prosper. If someone has done you wrong, don't try to correct it with another wrong because two wrongs will never make a right.

Once you know who you are (the infinite capacity to be) and why you are here (to discover this infinite capacity), envy, jealousy, resentment, and revenge become irrelevant. To master the troublesome four, be content, trustworthy, generous, and objective, and remember the world is real. It is your perception (how you see things) that is the illusion. Remove the maya (illusion), detach without indifference, and objectively see the world and all its events as opportunities to learn, know, and master your life; that's karma.

Change the way you see things and the way you see things changes.

Karma Plus the Troublesome Four

As we say with karma yoga—don't fall into D-GAP. As you move through life, while working on your karma each of the troublesome four will try and attach themselves to your work. If you let them, they will make your labor one of burden as opposed to joy.

Envy brings with it deceit, which causes us to confuse acquiring for achieving. **Many people are good at acquiring, but not at achieving.**

Greed brings a lack of contentment, while anger leaves us wanting to inflict misfortune (revenge) because our sense of pride is misdirected, and we feel inferior.

Jealousy is often disguised in deceiving ourselves into feeling threatened. Greed comes along to make us feel a loss of control, while anger adds suspicion and pride leaves us without trust.

Resentment's deceit is in blaming others and not taking responsibility for our part. Do we really think that we had nothing to do with the unfolding of events in our lives? Resentment gets attached to greed, leaving us measuring success by outward appearance while feeling angry because the world seems unfair and disappointing. Our pride kicks in to make us feel like victims.

Revenge deceives us by getting into our heads. We are the ones who suffer when we deceive ourselves with thoughts of greed fueled by anger and enhanced by self-deserving pride that seeks to even the score with an eye for an eye and a tooth for a tooth.

Be careful not to fall into D-GAP and be controlled by The Troublesome Four. Just be aware when they arrive. Trust me on this one, they will arrive, one by one, in a pair, and sometimes all together at once. Acknowledge them and then investigate why you let these eight get into your head and control your life in such a burdensome and impoverished way. What did you gain?

Deceit, greed, anger, and pride will never be mastered by letting envy, jealousy, resentment, and revenge reside in your mind.

Be careful what you let occupy your mind. Because what you let in your mind will occupy you.

CHAPTER FIFTEEN

The Nine Obstacles

Karma yoga teaches us that if we want to prosper, we must overcome the nine obstacles that impede our progress. Each obstacle must be examined and then counterbalanced, or worked through by developing the nine characteristics or qualities that allow us to overcome the nine obstacles. Pay attention to the ego awareness moment at the end of each obstacle.

First, we need to identify the nine obstacles.

The First Obstacle—Ill Health

You probably didn't get up this morning and think about how grateful you are to have good health and the ability to easily navigate through your life. That's because we take good health for granted until we lose it. Yoga teaches us that the first thing we should do every day is attend to our good health, for without it everything else is meaningless. Each day pay attention to the three pillars of health: diet, exercise, and sleep. These are the foundation for keeping the body and the mind healthy. Attitude and gratitude for the wonderful things the body can do should be our focus so that we stay healthy and fit. Remember, the soul is here to do its Earthly work and it needs a healthy body and healthy mind to do the job.

Consciously do what you can to prevent illness rather than take your health for granted. Karma yoga is about being consciously aware of all the things that you think, say, and do, and then acting in a way that creates the greatest good. Nothing in this world could be better than a healthy body and a healthy mind assisting the soul in completing its Earthly mission: having awareness of, and then overcoming, the obstacles of life from a peaceful healthy perspective.

EGO: flip your hands up and rest them on your knees. Extend out the index finger—the symbol of the ego. The ego fights for your survival. It strives to maintain its strength, but often confuses strength for power. In its power struggle to excel it often takes on stress and anxiety, leading to ill health. The ego fights to maintain its importance. Do not seek to extinguish the ego. It is for your self-preservation and self-identity. Simply seek to temper it by drawing your index finger in and placing your thumb on top which is the symbol of our soul. Take a breath and surrender to your soul. Remember that from the soul's perspective, we are here on Earth to overcome the obstacles of life. To overcome life's obstacles, continue to practice karma and focus on the three pillars of health: diet, exercise, and sleep. Practicing karma yoga, you will make great progress in your life. Through continual practice, you will learn how to overcome the many challenges and obstacles of life. Overcome ill health by making healthy choices.

The Second Obstacle—Boredom and Apathy

The second obstacle is what the Buddhists and Yogis call "sunyata," which means to be empty and void. This also means to have apathy and boredom.

The Nine Obstacles

Boredom and apathy can appear in many ways, but these are a few common experiences: lack of interest in activities, unable to stay interested in anything for more than brief periods, unable to rest and relax, no feeling of excitement, and difficulty staying motivated.

When we experience any or all of these, we feel unfulfilled and not able to feel a connection to our surroundings. Boredom can appear in two ways: being lethargic (feeling tired) or agitation (feeling irritated). And neither of these leads to happiness, fulfillment, and success.

Boredom is an emotion or signal that lets you know that you are doing something that doesn't give you satisfaction. Boredom could tell you two things: that you are not fully present and engaged in your current task, or that your task is not meaningful to you.

Quite prevalent in our modern world is the constant stimulation and searching for the next big thing and new experiences. These often get replaced with dull ambivalence. We get tired with the pursuit of our goals as they fall into over-stimulation or become routine.

In yoga, "tamas" is mind energy that arise from ignorance and prevent a person from finding their soulful path. Tamasic qualities are **laziness, anger, attachment, depression, dependency, self-doubt, guilt, boredom, irritation, addiction, apathy, confusion, grief, and ignorance**. When we replace them with enthusiasm and joy we find satisfaction, happiness, and success.

This is why yoga makes it the first order of business to tame the mind of its "chitta" (fluctuations) and find peace; to tame the mind be enthusiastic, focused, aware, and kind.

The first two obstacles to overcome on the pathway to soulful happiness and success are ill health and boredom. Neither of these will give you the vitality and enthusiasm for life. We are here to work our karma, and part of that work is to strive to overcome the obstacles of life. It is impossible to work your karma if you are ill and apathetic about life. But if you are healthy, energetic, and enthusiastic about your life, you will find that success and happiness are with you always. Appreciate life and you will live a satisfying and enriched life, and that is why we are here; to find happiness and joy.

EGO: Flip your palms up and extend out your index finger—the symbol of the ego. The ego wants satisfaction. But the ego is never satisfied. It always wants more. When you give the ego what it wants, it's only satisfied for a fraction of time before it starts to want more again. This causes us to get bored and apathetic.

Pull your index finger in and place your thumb on top—the symbol of your soul. Take a breath and surrender to your soul.

There is no right or wrong way to control your ego. Find what works for you. When you find what works, the key is consistency. When conflicts arise, take a moment to get quiet and listen to your inner voice. Be aware of what you are trying to achieve in your life. If it's joy, act accordingly. To overcome the obstacles of life, be healthy and be enthusiastic.

The Third Obstacle—Doubting Self Worth

The third obstacle is doubting your self-worth. One of the greatest obstacles to living an authentic, beautiful, and happy life is self-doubt. When we doubt our capacity to love, to say the right thing, to do good, and to be our authentic self, we live in fear of not being good enough. This binds us to the three basic fears in life: being rejected, being unloved, and dying.

Karma teaches us to observe life, and part of observing is examining how you think of yourself. We all have moments when we doubt ourselves. That usually happens when we look externally for validation rather than looking within. We let social media, family, coworkers, and those around us define what we wear, the behaviors we should adopt, and the beliefs we should uphold. That's why karma keeps reminding us that our work here is not about the material world, but about working on ourselves. According to karma, you chose this body and this life to discover, even in the midst of life's chaos and moments of self-doubt, the beautiful, unique individual inside of you.

To overcome self-doubt takes self-love and that takes work—that's karma!

The next time you're feeling inadequate, take a few minutes to quiet the world around you and take a breath. Loving yourself is the key to loving others and being the best you can be. Self-doubt can ruin so many of the beautiful things in life. It causes us to miss out on new work opportunities, giving back to others, and living freely. Taking a few small steps today to increase your self-love will banish doubt and help you grow in confidence.

EGO: Flip your palms up and extend your index finger—the symbol of your ego. Remember, your ego wants to protect you from getting hurt. This can be a good thing when faced with danger, but the deeper fears of not being accepted, of not being loved, and the fear of dying comes from a place of self-doubt. The ego forgets that the universe at its purest is a living, accepting, and loving place. Comparing yourself to others or questioning your abilities feeds into the ego's fear.

Pull your index finger in and place your thumb on top. Take a breath and surrender to your soul. The soul knows that we are all unique and on our own journey, while at the same time interconnected with everything and everyone in the world, for the sole purpose of working our karma, and part of working your karma is to overcome the obstacle of self-doubt. When it arises, and it will, just remember you are alive, so live fully, love yourself, and honor your self-worth. Once you overcome the obstacles of ill health, boredom, and self-doubt you are on the road to health, happiness, and peace, and that is what it means to live a successful life.

The Fourth Obstacle—Distractions and Carelessness

When we are distracted, we are often careless, and both of these lead to mistakes, injuries, and poor judgment. If we truly want to succeed in life, it requires focused effort and a careful approach. Without focus the mind becomes scattered, and a scattered mind is exactly what karma yoga teaches us needs to be tamed.

If you are trying to master something you must give it your focused attention, otherwise nothing is ever completed. We must also be careful with what we do with our energy, otherwise we waste time and effort and nothing gets accomplished. This can be detrimental to the health of the body, mind, and soul.

Yoga reminds us to be present and aware, always being careful about what we think, say, and do. This requires conscious awareness, and that is what it means to work your karma. If you are aware of the things that distract you and scatter your energy, you will be more careful about how you use your energy. Use it for the right purpose, at the right time, with the right amount of focus, and you will succeed.

Emotions, feelings, desires, and cravings scatter the life force, and when the life force is scattered it is difficult to find peace and tranquility. This of course takes work, and that is what it means to work your karma.

Life will always present us with obstacles to overcome. Awareness of these obstacles and the valuable lessons they teach us is working your karma. It is easy in today's world to get distracted by all that is happening in the world around you. That is why karma reminds us to still the mind and then to focus on the important things: your health, joy, enthusiasm, self-knowledge, and self-worth. Master these and be like the warrior; focus on your energy and then carefully use it at the right time, with the right amount of force, for the right purpose, and you will succeed.

EGO: Flip your palms up and extend the index finger—your ego. The ego is always looking here and there in the outside world for its worth, validation, and enthusiasm. The ego is constantly being distracted in its quest to both survive and thrive. It forgets that to survive in the world we need focus and caution. Distractions and carelessness can lead to stress and ill health, lack of enthusiasm, and self-doubt. Pull your index finger in and place your thumb on top. This is the symbol of the soul. Take a breath and surrender to the calmness of your soul. The soul reminds us to stop and think before we speak and before we act. When the mind is focused, we can direct our energy to create a more carefully directed life for ourselves and for the world at large. To do this remove distractions. Stay focused on what is important and be careful where and how you direct your energy. In this you will prosper.

The Fifth Obstacle—Unbridled Cravings and Desires

To begin with, there is nothing wrong with having desires. We are hardwired to seek pleasure. Without this we could not survive. We all desire to live a better and healthier life. But when desires become unbridled and obsessive and lead to cravings that distract us from our karmic work, they become an obstacle in the way of living a successful life, which means to have health, happiness, and peace in your body, mind, and soul.

When we have cravings and desires, they bind us and drive us to satisfy them. Once satisfied, we become somewhat peaceful until the next craving or desire arises. This keeps us in the perpetual cycle of discontentment. Karma teaches us to work on disciplining the subconscious mind so we might draw into it the thoughts found in the conscious mind. Here we are able to produce genuine contentment and peace. How? Quiet the mind and observe. The whole point of karma is to learn to be content and at peace with what comes into your life and what goes out of your life while observing and learning life's lessons.

When you have genuine happiness that is not attached to anything, you control cravings and desires, and this allows you to control your life. Nothing in the world binds you. Yoga reminds us that we can control the chitta (fluctuations) in our minds and that we control everything.

Be content with who you are, body, mind, and soul. Contentment is an inner peace independent of any external force. It means to be independently happy and satisfied no matter what enters or exits your life. When content, you are at peace with yourself and the world. When at peace with yourself and the world, it's easy to remove cravings and find satisfaction.

EGO: Flip your hands up and extend out your index finger; the symbol of your ego. The ego wants acceptance and importance. It sees those who have powerful titles and expensive cars and houses as more important than it is, and so it craves these things. It believes that these things symbolize acceptance, happiness, and success. And although power and wealth can make it appear that one's life is more important and easier, in the end, we take none of this with us. Cravings and desires can take on an addictive nature. This scatters the life force and keeps us in the perpetual cycle of seeking pleasure, but ultimately finding pain.

Pull your index finger in and place your thumb on top. Take a breath and surrender to your soul. When you have true contentment and happiness within, you are connected with your soul. Here it matters not what comes into your life or what leaves your life. The soul finds joy and appreciation in experiencing all of life just as it is in each moment.

The Sixth Obstacle—Feeling Heavy and Burnt Out

We all have feelings of exhaustion, stress, and overload from time to time, so karma reminds us to pay attention to these feelings. It's time to slow down and bring some balanced peace and tranquility back into your life so you can avoid the obstacle of becoming burnt out. It's hard to be energetic, enthusiastic, happy, and focused when faced with heavy feelings and exhausted. So, take some time and work on being present, balanced, tranquil, and peaceful.

The basis of life is energy, and it is what we do with our energy that determines whether we survive or perish. To overcome heaviness and becoming burnt out, we need to balance our energy body, mind, and soul, and that means to find harmony.

It is so easy to get caught up in the dramas and stressors of life and let them lead us to exhaustion. But the irony of life is that for all our outward strivings and all the dramas, in the end the sum total always adds up to zero. We take none of the dramas, problems, and stressors with us when we depart this world. What we do take is the compassion, understanding, and ability to observe and let go. Life is all about our experiences, and how we use our energy in each of these experiences determines whether we live a life of harmony or one strife with the heaviness and dramas that lead to becoming burnt out. Being burnt out is truly an obstacle when it comes to being healthy and finding peace and harmony. Let go, observe, and find balance. *Seek balance in all things and in all things find balance.*

EGO: Flip your palms up and extend out your index finger; the symbol of your ego. The ego is constantly striving to excel, to be important, and to consume. It wants acceptance and love. All of this comes from the citta, or the perceptions we hold in our mind. Pull your finger in and place your thumb on top. Take a breath and surrender to your soul. The soul sits back and watches as the mind, the ego, or the "I" strives to feel important and always be right. Once you begin to control the "I" and see it for what it really is: desire, cravings, distractions, worry, and self-doubt, you can begin to take control over your thoughts, knowing you can change them as you will; you are not bound by the dictates of the outside world. There is nothing wrong with the world. It is there for you to use it. You can make it a peaceful and harmonious place, or a heavy, dramatic, and exhausting place depending upon your approach. If you can control your mind you can control your energy, and when you control and direct your energy, you can create a world of harmony and balance. That is the antidote to being heavy and burnt out; an obstacle worth overcoming.

The Seventh Obstacle—Doubting One's Progress

This means to question or compare our lives to others. Here we might question why someone else is more successful, smarter, or more soulfully evolved. Have they made more progress in life than we have? We live in a world where it can appear that others are more successful and moving down life's path at a faster pace. We doubt our progress.

Have you ever questioned where you are or what you are doing with your life, and wondered if you were on the right path? This is a byproduct of the obstacle of self-doubt. When you doubt yourself, you doubt the progress you've made. Karma, however, teaches us that we are all on our individual paths and the markers of the material world are not an indicator of how far we have progressed soulfully.

The soul is here to turn deceit, greed, anger, and pride into truth, generosity, kindness, and humility. Awareness of this and taking this direction puts you further down the path than someone ignorant of what progress means. This does not mean that you cannot be wealthy and powerful. It's what you do with your energy that is the true marker of progress. Regardless of where you are, if you are working on being honest, generous, kind, and humble you are making progress in life. Takes work—that's karma.

Everyone faces doubt in varying intensities—from a subtle whisper to a loud emotional shout. Doubt, however, can remind us to go back to our most basic truth—love. Where there is true love, there is no doubt.

Doubt can teach us a thing or two about ourselves and the world. We have an opportunity to see where we lack trust, and as such, can make a different choice.

When we become aware of doubt, we connect to a deeper part of our being—a place of stillness and peace. Here we connect with the soul, or our essence, and it is here that we truly discover our progress along life's path. Trust and love yourself, be honest, generous, kind, and humble, and you will make tremendous progress in life.

EGO: Flip your palms up and extend the index fingers; the symbol of the ego. Doubt at its core is a fearful emotion. It is the ego shouting at us to take charge, as it fears not being accepted, or being rejected, and not being loved. It doubts its own self-worth and questions its progress. Pull your index finger in and place your thumb on top; the symbol of the soul. Take a breath and surrender to your soul.

When we surrender to the essence of our being, our soul, we discover that each path is unique. Comparison and competition do not fit into the soul's mission. The soul is here to help us quiet the mind and to see the world for what it really is—an opportunity to discover trust, generosity, kindness, and humility within ourselves, and when we discover these qualities within, we have no need to doubt ourselves or our progress.

Many times, we climb up hills only to slide down, or we climb to the top of the mountain only to realize we climbed the wrong mountain for the wrong reason. So, we must come down and begin a new climb. Takes continual practice to navigate life. Sometimes we get it right and sometimes we don't. But we need to keep practicing if we are to achieve prosperity with a purpose.

Karma yoga presents us with nine qualities or characteristics that will help us to overcome life's obstacles. Read on and use these to create a successful and fulfilling life.

The Eighth Obstacle—Getting Caught in the Illusion of Life

Getting caught in the illusion of life means to have a false impression of life as being a certain way, a false sense of security, and a false sense of importance.

Maya means illusion, or boundaries. Just remember that the world is made up of real experiences through which we might gain real knowledge into the nature of our purusha: *our real being known as the soul.*

Everything in the world is real. It is all here for our growth and evolution, but we forget and believe that acquiring things of the world is why we are here. We see the world though our own perspective, forgetting that everyone has a unique view of the world. We may share a common reality, but how we experience life and how we perceive life is unique to each of us. The illusion is in believing that how we perceive the world is the only view.

We often look to the material world to define us. It is not the material world that defines us, but what does define us is what we do with the material world, and how we do or do not let it build character, values, and virtues. The only thing that is permanent is what you cultivate within. That is why karma suggests we use the yamas and niyamas as guides.

Money, health, happiness, possessions, and relationships come and go, but the virtues you build within you carry through each incarnation. The world is real—how we perceive the world is the illusion. So, work to develop virtues within. Know the world is real and then use it as a great opportunity to build acceptance, tolerance, compassion, and understanding and you will overcome the obstacle of illusion. It takes work to separate yourself and see the world for what it is—an opportunity to master your karma.

Remember, everything in the world is real and ever changing. Nothing in life is permanent except the characteristics and qualities you develop and retain. Wealth, material things, world peace, technology, emotions, and feelings are all constantly changing. It is up to us to see the world for what it is; a great opportunity to sincerely appreciate the world as real while being fully aware of the uniqueness of every living being. When you can do this, you overcome the obstacle of illusion.

EGO: Flip your palm up and extend the index finger; the symbol of the ego. The ego is the part of us that identifies with the world. The maya, or the illusion, is in the mind. The mind gets scattered and cluttered with chitta (mind stuff). This drags us into believing the illusion; to having a false impression of life as being a certain way, a false sense of security, and a false sense of importance. Here we get caught in the illusion of life, and this can be a big obstacle to overcome when it comes to living a successful life.

Pull your finger in and place the thumb on top. Take a breath and surrender to your soul. The whole point of life is to bring together in perfect harmony the material world and the soulful essence. We are here to work the mission of the soul, which is to overcome the four great passions and the nine obstacles, so that we might find harmony and peace. The world is not an illusion. It is real and it is here for us to experience and gain knowledge so we might discover our true purpose.

Everything in the world is real. It is here for your evolution. The maya or illusion is in believing that everything is ego-related and real from the perspective of the ego. Use the world, but do not be used by it. Remember: you are a steward of life, so use it wisely. To overcome maya, detach without indifference. Withdraw and reflect with an objective point of view. Remove the emotional attachment and you will discover clarity. You will begin to understand why you are here and what you are here to learn. See every problem and decision as an opportunity to learn, know, and master your karma, and thus you master your life.

The world is not an illusion, it is made of real things and experiences so that we might have the opportunity to discover, define, and refine our purusha.

Life cannot be understood through intellectual interpretation. Life can only be understood through experiences. See the experiences for what they are: opportunities.

To compete in life requires a strong body and a steady mind, but to be successful requires something deeper; a sincere and intellectual understanding of maya.

The Ninth Obstacle—An Inability to Maintain Continual Practice

This means to remain steadfast and committed to something. If you want to succeed or master anything, you must practice, practice, and continue to practice. Without practice, nothing can be achieved. If you wish to achieve a state of vitality, happiness, and peace you will need to focus on your health, your self-worth, and seeing life for what it really is; an opportunity to learn, know, and master. This requires constant practice, otherwise we get careless and distracted by cravings and desires.

Everyday life will present you with obstacles to overcome. That is why you need to practice finding your balance, strength, flexibility, and peace. It takes work—that's karma!

Even after you have succeeded and mastered something, you must continue to practice. Karma yoga is a lifelong practice because it is about how you choose to live your life. This means to continually practice making conscious choices every moment you live.

The most important thing in your life is your health, followed by happiness and peace. Each of these takes continual practice. So, practice every day taking care of the most important things in life: your health, body, mind, and soul.

EGO: Flip up your palm and extend out your index finger; the symbol of the soul. The ego thinks itself the master, forgetting that it is the reflection of the true self filtered through the mind. Karma teaches that the true self is selfless. But when filtered through the perceptions and attitudes of the mind, it has a tendency to become selfish. It often gets caught in the illusion of life, boosting its own importance.

Pull your index finger in and place your thumb on top. Take a breath and surrender to the symbol of the soul.

At the core we are our selfless essence or our true self, which is pure, simple, and unique. It's independent of the body and the mind, and yet depends upon the body-mind for its existence here on Earth. Life will present us with many obstacles. It takes continual practice to overcome and master life's obstacles. Practice, practice, and keep practicing.

CHAPTER SIXTEEN

Nine Qualities and Characteristics to Develop

What are Character and Qualities?
 To overcome obstacles and challenges requires the development of certain characteristics and qualities. These are traits or attributes of an individual that define their personality, behavior, and outlook on life. Every individual possesses a unique set of characteristics that have been shaped by their life experiences, environment, and culture. The ability to recognize and cultivate positive characteristics and qualities in oneself can lead to personal growth and success in various aspects of life.

Karma yoga views characteristics and qualities as ways to progress along the pathway to soulful growth, self-realization, and prosperity. According to yoga, we all possess what are called the "gunas." These fall into three categories. The first is *"sattva,"* which is purity, goodness, and kindness as well as wisdom, compassion, love, and harmony. The second is "rajas," the quality of activity and restlessness. It is associated with ambition, passion, greed, and desire. The third is "tamas," the quality of laziness and inertia. Its characteristics are ignorance, laziness, depression, and apathy. To overcome obstacles, we need to develop the sattva and reduce the rajas and tamas. With the practice of karma yoga, we work towards developing sattva; more positive characteristics and qualities in ourselves. This can lead to greater self-awareness, inner peace, and soulful growth. These characteristics are important if you wish to prosper.

To bring more sattva into your life, align yourself with and focus on developing kindness, purity, wisdom, compassion, love, and harmony. Remember: what you think, say, and do reflects the characteristics and qualities you have developed. You have the power to change 84 percent of who you are. You cannot change your individuality or your family of origin, but you do have the power to change your beliefs and attitudes, especially if they do not align with what brings health, happiness, and peace to your life.

According to karma, our characteristics and qualities are not our true nature, but rather a set of patterns and tendencies we have developed throughout our lives. These are attached to the ego. The ego is what gives us a sense of individuality and separates us from others, but it is also what can lead to attachment, suffering, and prevent us from achieving self-realization and soulful growth. The ego is the false sense of self that identifies with the characteristics of righteousness, importance, and attachment.

Karma teaches us how to detach from the ego (if only for a moment) by recognizing that our characteristics and qualities are not who we truly are. They are byproducts of our experiences. How we develop and use these characteristics determines the outcome of our lives. We are here on Earth as curious souls here to learn and understand life, and with that comes characteristics.

If the need to be right or self-importance should arise, take a breath, step away from the ego, and connect with your soul. It will encourage you to control the four great passions and then to cultivate qualities such as selflessness, kindness, compassion, and humility. These will make your life harmonious and peaceful. Who wouldn't want that?

To overcome obstacles, pay attention to your character—it matters.

The First Characteristic

The first characteristic karma suggests we work to develop is the ability to be calm. Calmness means having tranquil and balanced energy in our body, mind, and soul. It involves being free from stress and anxiety and being able to think and act in a clear and composed manner.

Calmness is considered an essential part of inner growth, clarity, and a quiet mind. It allows you to think and act more rationally and to overcome the obstacles of distraction and carelessness. Being calm enables you to make better decisions, solve problems, and handle stress more appropriately. With less tension, stress, and anxiety we connect better with other people and the world around us.

Think for a moment what it would be like if all around you there was chaos, stress, and overload, and yet you could remain calm. This of course would take a lot of conscious effort, and that is karma; being conscious of your thoughts, words, and actions and how they can affect an outcome.

Developing the characteristic of calmness through yoga involves training the mind to be present, letting go of distractions and attachments, and focusing on finding balance in body, mind, and soul. Practicing calmness in yoga, we use the physical poses to take tension out of the body, which also requires the mind to be present. To remove anything, such as tension, you must be focused.

As the body lets go of tension, so the mind becomes quiet, and when we do that, we bring a sense of calmness to our lives. If we continue the practice, over time this state of calmness will positively impact our daily lives, our relationships, and our overall wellbeing in our body, mind, and soul.

Look for those moments where you encounter problems, chaos, and stress as opportunities to be calm, and when you do, you will be working your karma and will prosper.

Calmness is a quality that helps us to overcome life's obstacles without losing our balance. We are here to develop punja, or virtuous characteristics that enhance our life. We have the power to choose who we want to be. We do this by building character and qualities such as calmness. Just remember, all of life is simply a process of making decisions and solving problems. Calmness allows us to do a better job at both. Calmness is a good quality to have.

EGO: Flip your palms up and extend out the index finger; the symbol of your ego. The ego makes decisions based upon emotions rather than logic. It wants to be in control and to always be right. It also likes to feel superior or entitled.

Pull your finger in and place your thumb on top. Take a breath and surrender to your soul. Free of agitation and disturbance, calmness is associated with inner peace, self-worth, and self-acceptance. On a soulful level, calmness is believed to be the result of connecting with a higher power and allowing the universe to take its course. It is a reminder to trust in ourselves, the path we are on, and be open to all the possibilities that come our way.

Be calm—it will serve you well.

The Second Characteristic

The second characteristic to develop is self-discipline. Our world operates in a regulated and disciplined way. Without discipline, nothing can be achieved. If everything was chaotic, life could not progress. If the sun, moon, and Earth did not rotate in a disciplined way, we would not have the calculations to send rockets and satellites into space.

Nature is disciplined; it does not try to be something it is not. It is only humans who think they can do anything they want without consequences, and this creates chaos.

Self-discipline doesn't mean to live an austere life. It means to know your limits and then to stop before you cross over and lose your balance.

Karma yoga is more than an exercise for the body. If practiced with self-discipline, you will find that it affects your entire being body, mind, and soul. When you are attempting to improve your life, self-discipline is needed. Self-improvement begins by doing the best you can with what you have. Start where you are and watch your attitude; it is tied to self-discipline.

Regular practice is required if you are to achieve anything, and this requires self-discipline. Failing to continue any discipline or practice is one of the obstacles to success. You can't be successful at anything unless you commit the time and the energy to it, and that takes discipline.

When you practice discipline, you get a greater sense of happiness, contentment, and wisdom. That is because self-discipline brings a sense of calmness, structure, and order to your life.

Everything in the universe must be fed. If a dream or a goal is fed daily, eventually it will become a reality. But we must have the self-discipline to continue to feed it or it will die. All that is born within the world carries within it the seed of (process) dissolution. If not fed, it will dissolve. So, if you hope to achieve anything in life, it requires the quality of self-discipline.

EGO: Flip up your palms and extend out your index finger; the symbol of the ego. The ego loves instant gratification. Sometimes it thinks it is smarter than nature and doesn't need to implement self-discipline. Sometimes it even takes pride in its false sense of discipline and believes it has nothing left to improve. Bring your finger in and place the thumb on top. Take a breath and surrender to the soul. Self-improvement begins by doing the best you can with what you have. To achieve anything, you must have self-discipline. You are what you think, say, and do, so watch your attitude; it is tied very closely to your sense of self-worth and self-discipline. Self-discipline is a good quality to have.

Even good deeds will bind you if you do them for egotistical gratification.

The Third Characteristic

Karma yoga views characteristics and qualities as ways to progress along the pathway to soulful growth and self-realization.

The third characteristic is to be able to withdraw and reflect. To withdraw means to remove oneself from a situation or to disengage from your surroundings both physically and mentally. Reflecting involves introspection and self-examination. It means to reflect upon your thoughts, words, and actions in order to gain insight and understanding.

In yoga, we call this sense withdrawal, which means to turn inward so that we can quiet the mind, create a sense of inner calmness, and then make positive changes in our lives. If we combine this with self-study or reflection, we gain self-awareness and self-knowledge. Karma reminds us that one of the obstacles to a peaceful, successful, and happy life is blocking our feelings. When we block our feelings, we block our self-awareness.

Withdrawing and reflecting means to control the senses. The senses are like a mirror. By themselves they are pure and innocent. Turn them outward and they reflect the turbulent and chaotic world. Turn them inward and the mirror reflects our state of being. The world is a battlefield. When we look outside, we must always be prepared to fight against deceit, greed, anger, and pride. When we withdraw, reflect, and look inside, we will also be challenged by the battles of life, but if we practice calmness with reflection, we can find quietude, peace, and happiness. Look inward, withdraw, reflect, and create a state of being that reflects your ability to be calm and disciplined and you will build strong and worthy characteristics.

EGO: Flip your palms up and extend out the index fingers; the symbol of the ego. The ego easily deludes itself by comparing itself to others while believing it has control over itself even while putting in very little effort. But any minute there can be a slip up and the mind can lose control and the ego will find itself on the battlefield of life fighting for survival. Pull your fingers in and place your thumbs on top, take a breath, and surrender to the soul. The soul knows how to withdraw and reflect. Like a mirror turned inward, reflect upon your true and pure state of being. It reminds us that if we find and cultivate the quality of peace within, we will find peace wherever we go.

The Fourth Characteristic

The fourth characteristic is tranquility, which means to have the stature or poise to hold still and contemplate before you speak or act.

Tranquility is a state of calmness, peacefulness, and serenity. It means to be free of agitation, anxiety, and chitta, or fluctuations of the mind. Tranquility can be experienced in a peaceful natural environment, through meditation, or by engaging in activities that promote relaxation and stress reduction, such as yoga.

Physically, tranquility lowers the heart rate, decreases muscle tension, and creates a sense of lightness and ease in the body, as well as mental and emotional calmness. We move without effort and with ease.

Tranquility involves contemplation, which is a mental practice that involves focusing on a particular subject or idea with the intention of gaining a deeper insight. It can be from meditation or used for secular purposes such as solving problems, making decisions, and creative inspiration.

Karma yoga describes tranquility as the ability to hold still, quiet the mind, and then contemplate (think calmly) before you speak or act. It's not an easy thing to do, it takes work—that's karma!

Taking time to cultivate tranquility and engage in contemplation can have many positive effects on your mental and physical wellbeing, such as reducing stress and preventing burnout. It can be a very valuable practice or characteristic to incorporate into you daily routine. Tranquility makes problems easier to solve and decisions easier to make.

Some of the obstacles you need to overcome in order to achieve a successful life are stress, burnout, lack of focus, poor decision-making, and lack of self-worth. When you practice tranquility and contemplation you can reduce stress, gain the ability to focus, make better decisions, become more self-aware, increase creativity, and generally make an impact on your health in body, mind, and soul. Tranquility would be a good characteristic to develop.

EGO: Flip your palms up and extend out the index fingers; the symbol of the ego. The ego runs here and there always looking at things external to itself. Without going inward it can never know it's true self, and so it feels anxious, stressed, and exhausted. When we stop, get tranquil, and quietly connect ourselves to the world we occupy, we have an opportunity to realize that our view of the world is not necessarily the only and right view. Pull your fingers in, place your thumbs on top, take breath, and surrender your ego to your soul. Sitting quietly, remember contemplation can help you recognize your own limitations. This can foster a sense of humility, which can improve our relationships with others and allow us to be more open to gaining new knowledge. We are here to master our lives and make peace within. Tranquility and contemplation would be good characteristics to have.

The Fifth Characteristic

The fifth quality or characteristic is to have a sincere and intellectual appreciation for life.

Intellect and appreciation are integral to the practice of karma yoga, as they help to cultivate gratitude, selfless actions, and detachment from outcomes. We do something because it is good for all, and not just good for us as individuals.

To have sincere and intellectual appreciation for life, one must develop understanding and respect for the natural world, human relationships, and oneself. This means to recognize the interconnectedness of all things as well as understanding the impact or effect of one's actions, and then striving to make a positive contribution to the world.

A sincere and intellectual appreciation for life means recognizing and valuing the significance of one's existence and the world around them in a thoughtful and authentic way. It involves being aware and grateful for the opportunities and experiences that life presents, as well as acknowledging the difficulties and challenges that come with it.

To practice karma yoga means to take actions that are motivated by a desire to serve others and contribute to the greater good of humanity. It all begins with your ability to find balance, strength, flexibility, and peace in a chaotic world.

A sincere and intellectual appreciation for life means approaching life with an open mind, seeking to learn and grow from our experiences and to embrace the uncertainty and impermanence of existence. Ultimately, having a sincere and intellectual appreciation for life is about finding meaning and purpose in one's own life and then contributing to the good of humanity.

Intellect and appreciation for life are essential to karma yoga, which is a soulful practice that emphasizes calmness, soulful reflection, discipline, and tranquility.

Appreciation means recognizing the value and significance of every moment and every being, and then cultivating a deep sense of gratitude for the opportunities and experiences that life presents. By appreciating our experiences, we gain a sense of purpose and joy, and this leads to a prosperous life.

EGO: Flip your palms up and extend out the index fingers; the symbol of the ego. The ego plays a crucial role in how we perceive things, including our attachment to people, objects, and ideas. This can influence how we conduct our lives, such as identifying with our emotional attachments even when they are unhealthy. Fear of losing our attachments can cause us to over-identify with our emotions. For example, when we feel jealousy or rejection in response to a friend or relative spending time with someone else. We overly invest in these emotions, which causes us to cling to them and have a difficult time letting go.

Pull your index fingers in and place your thumbs on top, the symbol of the soul. Take a breath and surrender to the soul. Appreciation cultivates wisdom, and wisdom teaches us that the true nature of reality is that everything, even our emotions, are impermanent and constantly changing. When we sincerely and intellectually appreciate life, we cultivate selfless action, gratitude, and detachment from outcomes. Sincerely and intellectually appreciate all of life. It is here for your evolution.

The Sixth Characteristic

The sixth characteristic is to be able to endure suffering and hardships.

Life is filled with suffering, but it is also full of wonder, giving us many opportunities to endure and rise above suffering and hardships. There will always be suffering, hardships, losses, pain, anguish, and fear.

To endure suffering and hardships means to persist through difficult and challenging circumstances without giving up. It involves facing and overcoming adversity, even when it may be painful or uncomfortable. This requires mental and emotional strength, resilience, and perseverance. It involves recognizing that challenges and struggles are a natural part of accepting life and may be necessary for our personal growth and development.

For example, karma teaches us that if someone hurts us and this causes suffering and hardship, we should accept this as an opportunity to find within ourselves inner peace and liberation. By emotionally detaching from the pain of insults, abuses, and suffering, we have the opportunity to find within ourselves compassion and understanding. In this we learn to work our karma.

Once a man wanted to anger a saint, so he insulted him and called him names. The saint sat quiet and still. The man screamed, "Don't you understand what I am saying about you?"

The saint answered, "Yes."

And then the man yelled, "Then how can you sit there so quiet and still?"

The saint answered, "Suppose you brought me some fruit and I refused it. What would you do?"

"I would take it back," said the man.

"In the same way I refuse to accept the things you have called me, so you may take them back," he replied.

Karma yoga is a holistic approach to addressing suffering and hardships by integrating physical, mental, and soulful energy. This requires the ability to find balance, strength, flexibility, and peace in a chaotic and sometimes difficult world.

Even though life can be hard and full of suffering and hardships, we must try to focus on the good, the lessons, and the growth. To endure suffering and hardships, you must develop a great deal of courage, patience, and determination. Draw on your inner resources, such as faith, hope, and a sense of purpose, to help you through difficult times. Life is chaotic. Sufferings and hardships are part of human life. They will not disappear.

Like the saint, practice liberation; refuse to let them destroy your inner sense of peace. In this you will know what it means to work your karma.

EGO: Flip your palms up and extend out the index fingers; the symbol of the ego. The ego is our psyche. It is our sense of self and identity and can play a significant role in how we deal with suffering and hardships. The ego sometimes identifies with suffering, seeing it as a fundamental aspect of our identity. This can lead to victimization or self-pity, and this may intensify suffering. The ego may compare suffering to that of others either to minimize our own pain or to magnify it. This creates a feeling of superiority or inferiority. The ego seeks to control difficult experiences by trying to fix them or find a solution. While taking action may be helpful, the ego can get overly attached to control and may struggle to accept a situation that cannot be changed, intensifying the suffering and hardship.

Pull your index fingers in and place your thumbs on top, the symbol of the soul. Take a breath and surrender to the soul. The soul is the deepest aspect of our being. It is the source of meaning, purpose, and connection to something greater than our ego self. The soul responds to suffering with compassion and understanding by recognizing that all of life is interconnected and that we all share the joys and sorrows of life. Rather than being a victim, the soul finds meaning in suffering and hardships, using them for personal growth, learning, and transformation. The soul draws upon a deep sense of faith to endure suffering and hardship, and in this finds peace. This characteristic will help you find inner strength and to overcome self-doubt, cravings, illness, and illusion.

The Seventh Characteristic

The seventh characteristic is to be able to discriminate between right and wrong.

This is where ethics and morals come into play. Knowing the difference between right and wrong is not always crystal clear. It involves a combination of innate moral intuitions, societal norms, personal values, and ethical reasoning.

For example: we would all say it is wrong to steal. But if your children are dying of starvation, is it right or wrong to steal so they don't die? Karma reminds us above all else do no harm, but always do what does the greatest good for the greatest many.

Humans possess an inherent sense of empathy and fairness, which provides a framework for establishing what is right and what is wrong. However, these may vary somewhat among individuals and across different cultures.

Yoga provides us with a guideline for living an ethical life through the yamas and niyamas. The yamas call upon us to practice nonviolence, truthfulness, non-stealing, moderation, and non-greed. The niyamas remind us to observe purity, contentment, self-discipline, self-study, and to surrender to our higher power.

"Ahimsa," or nonviolence, is a fundamental principle of yoga. It means to refrain from doing any harm to oneself, others, and all living beings through physical actions, as well as speech and thoughts. But even yoga recognizes that the line between what is right and what is wrong is not always clear. For example, we are to do no harm and always tell the truth. But this can sometimes put us in a dilemma.

Once, on an early winter's day, a yogi was meditating in the woods. A beautiful deer ran by and jumped past him. Reflecting, the yogi thought how beautiful and graceful the deer was.

Soon after, a hunter came by and asked the yogi if he had seen the deer. If the yogi tells the hunter the truth about where the deer ran to, the hunter will kill the deer, and harm will be done. But winter is setting in and if he does not tell the truth, the hunter and his family will starve. This will create a greater harm. What should the yogi do? What is the right action and what is the wrong action? Here we see the dilemma between telling the truth and practicing nonviolence. The line between right and wrong is not always clear. Karma reminds us to always do what is the greatest good for the greatest many.

Yoga is a philosophical tradition that offers insight into the concept of right and wrong. Yoga places emphasis on withdrawal and self-reflection so that we might be more self-aware of how we conduct ourselves in our thoughts, words, and deeds. The line between what is right and what is wrong is not always clear. However, yoga encourages us to lead a life of nonviolence, integrity, and honesty. This means to be truthful, respectful, and fair. Align yourself with your higher principles; always do what is the greatest good for the greatest many while not harming yourself, others, and the world. This is one of the great challenges of life.

EGO: Flip your palms up and extend out your index fingers; the symbol of the ego. The ego always wants to be right because it is closely tied to our self-image, identity, and the need for validation. The ego likes control and approval and fears being wrong. It tends to favor information that affirms it beliefs and ignores or dismisses anything that contradicts it. This can blur the line between right and wrong.

Pull your index fingers in and place your thumbs on top; the symbol of the soul. Take a breath and surrender to the soul. When it comes to right and wrong, let your soul be your guide.

Be aware, withdraw, and self-reflect. The soul will remind you that we are all connected as one, and that we must be very careful with our interpretation of what is right and what is wrong. The soul will always seek to do what is right through the basic principle of do no harm, while remembering to always do what is the greatest good for the greatest many. Let your conscience (soul) be your guide.

Wisdom is in knowing the right path to take. Integrity is taking it.

The Eighth Characteristic

The eight characteristic is to have unfathomable faith. Karma yoga refers to unfathomable faith as a deep unwavering faith in one's ability to self-realize and soulfully grow even in the face of adversity. Having faith in one's abilities and potential leads to inner wisdom; an understanding that the path of life is not always easy, but if you have an unwavering faith in yourself, you will not only survive, but you will thrive.

Karma teaches us that every individual has the potential to tap into their inner strengths and to develop self-awareness, self-healing, and personal growth. Within all of us is the ability to overcome life's obstacles, as well as master the great passions: deceit, greed, anger, and pride.

Karma recognizes the presence of a higher power or divine energy that exists within and beyond the individual. We call this "Ishvar," or an absolute and total dedication of all your thoughts, words, and deeds to your chosen ideal in life. Unfathomable faith requires the ability to surrender to this higher power by truly listening and trusting your inner voice and letting it be your guide.

Nine Qualities and Characteristics to Develop

Unfathomable faith means commitment and dedication even during challenging times. There will be many challenges in life and obstacles to overcome, but when we remove self-doubt and replace it with steadfastness and perseverance, we will find the power to achieve. But it takes practice—that's karma!

Unfathomable faith is not just religious or spiritual beliefs, it's also means to have faith in our ability to navigate the many challenges and obstacles of life. Relationships, careers, families, and life in general requires a certain sense of faith if we are to succeed. Faith provides us with strength, resilience, determination, and the motivation to pursue our goals even when the path forward may seem uncertain. Faith surpasses ordinary limits and persists despite the obstacle of self-doubt. Have faith in yourself.

EGO: Flip your palms up and extend out your index fingers; the symbol of the ego. While unfathomable faith can be a source of inspiration and guidance, it can also lead to closed mindedness, dogmatism, and an unwillingness to consider alternative perspectives. The ego is very good at believing that its point of view is the only point of view, discounting alternative beliefs and perspectives. Pull your fingers in and place your thumbs on top; the symbol of the soul. Take a breath and surrender to your soul. When we take the time to connect with our soul, we are reminded to maintain a balance between holding onto our faith and being open to new ideas and different points of view. We are reminded to not get caught up in believing one way is right and another is wrong. Faith means to believe in yourself and follow your path, but always remember to do no harm to yourself, to others, or to Mother Earth.

The Ninth Characteristic

The ninth characteristic or quality karma suggests we should try to develop is striving to be the perfect human being. This means to be true to yourself, without doing harm, while equally disseminating the energy of health, happiness, and peace to all. Notice the word strive. It means to devote your energy towards achieving or obtaining something. With great effort and devotion, you can cause things to happen, and that is how to best use the energy of karma. Karma means selfless work. It means to work, not for accolades or material possessions, but to strive to better yourself, and as such to make the world a better place. But of course, that means you need to start by working on yourself.

Be true to yourself. Work to connect with and understand your true essence, or what makes you uniquely you. What makes you healthy, happy, and peaceful? What brings you great joy? When you are true to yourself, harmonious energy will flow through your life. You will prosper with a purpose. Seek to create wellbeing as opposed to harm, and equally wish everyone good health, pure joy, and a peaceful passage through life. This takes devotion and continual practice—that's karma!

What is perfection? By its very nature it is subjective. It is sometimes described as a flawless state without any shortcomings. However, karma teaches us that humans are inherently flawed and designed to make mistakes. We hopefully learn from our mistakes and then strive to correct them. Our imperfections, and we all have them, are the unique qualities that make us human and contribute to the diversity of life. Karma reminds us that we are here as imperfect humans to strive for perfection by working on our own corrections. Nowhere does karma teach that perfection is found in attributes such as beauty, intelligence, or ability. We are here to work our karma, and that means to strive to be the very best we can while embracing the idea that we are all a part of the greater whole, and when we can do that, we realize that the perfected human being is true to themselves, does no harm, and equally disseminates the energy of health, happiness, and peace to all. Be truthful, generous, kind, and humble.

EGO: Flip your hands up and extend out the index fingers; the symbol of the ego. The ego lives through fears of being rejected, not being accepted, not being loved, and death. So, it seeks validation and approval to prove to itself that it is perfect. We compare ourselves to others and compete with others in an attempt to feel superior and more successful. The ego sets unrealistic standards in its pursuit of an idealized perfect self-image, and when we fall short of this, we experience disappointment and despair. Often, the ego will strive to present a flawless façade to maintain a positive self-image and avoid judgement or criticism from others. The ego also tends to cling to a rigid identity, resisting growth or challenges, afraid of losing its perceived perfection.

Pull your index fingers in and place your thumbs on top; the symbol of the soul. Take a breath and surrender to your soul. The ego's definition of perfection can be limiting and potentially lead to feelings of inadequacy, stress, and a constant need for validation. The souls' definitions of perfection mean to liberate yourself from the attachment of the ego by freeing oneself from fear, desires, and illusions that hinder soulful growth.

From the soul's perspective, we are all perfect when we are true to ourselves and realize our inherent potential to create harmony, compassion, love, and empathy towards ourselves and others. Perfection is seen as an ongoing journey of self-discovery.

It involves the recognition and embodiment of gratitude, wisdom, forgiveness, and inner peace. It means to live your life in accordance with truthfulness, kindness, and integrity.

Nowhere does the soul define perfections in physical, mental, or material attributes. Perfection means to be true to yourself, do no harm, and equally disseminate the energy of health, happiness, and peace to all. Be true to yourself, for you have everything required to be the perfect soul.

Obstacles and Characteristics

Life will present you with nine obstacles: ill health, boredom and apathy, self-doubt, being scattered and careless, doubting your progress, uncontrolled cravings, allowing yourself to get heavy and burnt out, getting caught in the maya or illusion, and failing to continue a practice.

Each of these will impede your progress, but if you take the time to develop the nine characteristics of calmness, self-discipline, withdraw and reflect, tranquility and contemplation, sincere and intellectual appreciation for life, endure suffering and hardships, discriminate between what is right and what is wrong, have unfathomable faith, and strive to be the perfected human being, you will not only overcome life's obstacles, but you will prosper with purpose. But of course, this all takes conscious work. That's karma. *Life becomes what life does.*

One of the great illusions of life is in believing that mistakes, in general, make a person worthless and less than perfect. Just remember: the perfected human being is true to themselves, and that means living a life that is full of experiences so that we might evolve, and part of those experiences is making mistakes.

One day when I was young, I went to my father crying and told him I kept making mistakes and I did not know what to do. He looked me in the eye and said, "Do you think you have a design on making mistakes? Do you think you own the pattern? Everyone makes mistakes. Learn from them and move on."

In the words of John W. Gardner:

"Life is the art of drawing without an eraser."

CHAPTER SEVENTEEN

Soul Walking –
The pathway of prosperity with a purpose

The genesis for Soul Walking began in a very dark and almost hopeless time in my life. I found myself alone, struggling financially, and questioning every decision I had ever made. I had failed at finding my soul mate, my business ventures had all failed, and I was approaching forty. I asked myself why I was not able to find success. Where was the wealth, happiness, love, and freedom I so wanted? What was I doing wrong?

It has been said that from the darkest of moments comes the spark of inspiration. And so, from this dark place I had an epiphany. I was not being true to myself! It wasn't that I was a failure. I just wasn't following my true soulful path. I needed to discover my purpose and meaning for being in this life, and so I began what I call Soul Walking.

What I discovered on my soul walk was that prosperity is everywhere. The challenges and obstacles of life are simply opportunities to prosper; they are not barriers unless you make them so. If you ask the world to bring you prosperity, it will. If you ask it to bring you poverty, it will surely oblige. But either way it takes work, and that is the true nature of karma.

It was at this time, while working on my karma, that I stumbled upon an ancient yoga text about a lesser-known branch of yoga called Padmini Vidya—the pathway to prosperity. As I began to study and teach it in relationship to karma, I discovered that if you aim your life in four directions while paying careful attention to what you think, say, and do, you will discover the "nidhis" or the treasures of life, and if used in the proper manner they will bring you prosperity.

What is life all about? What does it mean and how can I find my purpose? We all want to know the answers, and when we don't know, neuroscientists tell us that this uncertainty creates a negative impact on the brain. When confronted with a situation that is contrary to our values, things can get uncertain, and this uncertainty leads to the perception of a threat. Threat, of course, creates stress. However, our brains are hardwired to avoid threat and/or move toward reward. That is why we are the happiest when we have a purpose and can find meaning in our lives. Knowing your purpose therefore creates a positive impact on the body, the mind, and the soul. But it is not enough just to find your purpose. You must then understand how to develop your purpose if you are to prosper and be successful. This requires following a prescribed set of steps known as **SOUL WALKING.**

The primary goal of yoga is expansion of consciousness into our highest potential. To do this, we need to understand how to use life's energy. We do this by having an inclination towards certain actions and a detachment from others, for which we need to harness the energy of the ego. The ego is the "I" that sits above the "me." It is necessary for self-preservation, but often confuses us into believing that the ego's point of view is the final view of reality. When we master the power of the ego and begin to harness and redirect its energy, we can remove the obstacles blocking our progress and enhance the merits that lead us to a successful life. By enhancing merits, the consciousness expands, and with this expansion of potential comes a greater ability to deal with the problems of everyday life, which is necessary if we are to prosper.

Yoga has many practices. Hatha yoga teaches us to take care of our body. Karma yoga teaches us how to embrace our work and make corrections. Anna teaches us how eat healthy. Bhakti teaches us how to be devoted. Tantra teaches us how to develop the creative spirit. Jnana teaches us how to foster wisdom. The less familiar branch of yoga, called Padmini Vidya, teaches us how to become prosperous so that we can make our lives and the world a better place.

Padmini Vidya is the science of the subtle forces used to attract wealth and thus success. But wealth is not just about the accumulation of money and material goods. It is about the active and willful control of the energy of consciousness to one's benefit. This is the greatest source of wealth. Follow Padmini Vidya and you will prosper.

Here are the three steps to success. Follow these and you will prosper:

Step One

Consciously control the direction of your willpower. But what is willpower? Having gratitude for what you have rather than constant desire for what you don't have is the first step. Put your attention on what you have and be grateful. When you are grateful you appreciate, and when you appreciate you move with grace, which creates a sense of *refinement as you move through life*. Reach out to develop your highest potential and pay attention to how gracefully you move through the space you occupy. Dwell in a state of prosperity and you will dwell in a conscious state of wealth energy. But this is more than pure positive thinking. This stream of energy can reshape your life in either positive or negative ways depending upon how you use it. Wealth can bestow great power, while misuse will surely make a person suffer. The universe has a perfect accounting system. No deed goes unnoticed. Master your willpower.

Step Two

Apply the following success formula towards your desired goal. You must have a vision or focus along with the desire to create. You must be willing to work diligently with consistency and persistence at a well-developed plan to achieve the results.

The formula is:

Vison+ desire+ plan+ consistency +persistency = success.

All of this must be backed with a positive stream of prosperity consciousness if you are to prosper. Hold steady to this formula but stay flexible, aware, and able to adjust as needed.

Step Three

Create punya, which means merits earned through our actions in this life and our past lives. When we see people who are wealthy and successful, the Buddhists and the Hindus would call this punya that was earned from good deeds in a past life. We in the Western world might call it luck. Karma yoga calls it the "good" karma you have earned from your past lives, as well as the merits you are earning in this life.

If we want to create punya we must exhaust papa, which means demerit or bad karma. Remember, karma attaches itself to our actions, our thoughts, and our speech. So, we need to be consciously aware of how our actions, thoughts, and speech affect our life. Papa might appear as dishonesty, disturbance, evil, worthlessness, demerit, fault, or weakness. Work to remove these and replace them with truthfulness, generosity, kindness, and humility.

The three basic methods for developing merits or punya are:
1. Giving without expecting a return
2. Living a virtuous life
3. Spreading good will

These fall in line with the ten ways to make merits. They are:
1. Give
2. Observe virtue
3. Concentration
4. Focus
5. Honor others
6. Be of service
7. Dedication
8. Be happy for others' good fortune
9. Listen to and practice virtuous teaching
10. Instruct others in being virtuous

Every obstacle in life is an opportunity to reveal the secret treasures of life. When you know where to find them and how to use them in conjunction with working your karma, you'll begin to understand what Lakshmi means by the four aims: wealth, pleasure, harmony, and liberation.

Now it is time for me to share with you that which I have learned through my practice, come to know through my writing, and mastered through my teaching.

CHAPTER EIGHTEEN

The Energy of Prosperity—RECAP

Everything in life is a byproduct of energy. Therefore, if we wish to be successful in life, we must learn how to harness the energy of prosperity. In Hinduism, *Shakti* is believed to be the cosmic energy that moves through the entire universe creating ability, strength, power, potential, and capacity. Shakti energy is the force that both maintains the universe and makes it disintegrate. Shakti is known as the spouse of Shiva, the Hindu God responsible for creation, upkeep, and the destruction of the world. Together they enter into a dance of creation and destruction. This energy is believed to lie dormant within each of us at the base of our spine, waiting to be awoken and lifted to our highest level of consciousness where we realize we are both the creative and destructive energy of our own lives.

As discussed in Chapter Seven, Padmini Vidya is the yoga of prosperity. "Padmini" means lady of the lotus and "vidya" means the science of yoga. The lady of the lotus refers to Lakshmi, the goddess of wealth and purity.

Lakshmi is personified as the shakti energy, and is also the wife of Vishnu, one of the principal deities of Hinduism. Vishnu protects all humans and restores order to the world. He is found in all aspects of creation, as well as destruction and regeneration. Together they enter into the dance that either creates or destroys. Used wisely, their energy will protect and regenerate. This cosmic dance, which we are all a part of, has the potential to create prosperity.

Lakshmi, the Goddess energy of prosperity, is a powerful force. Her name means "aim" or "goal." She has four arms, which signify her power to grant the four goals or directions towards a successful and prosperous life: wealth (hat), worldly pleasure (kama sutra), harmony by adhering to a good moral and ethical code (dharma), and soulful liberation (moksha).

These four goals grant us a fulfilling and prosperous life. The aim of the goals is to direct your highest potential into creating a prosperous and wealthy life.

Lakshmi symbolizes prosperity and well-being and is honored by many. She teaches us the Padmini Vidya, or the yoga of prosperity. Prosperity is seen as good and necessary for a healthy and successful society, as well as for the individual. Surprisingly, only a small fraction of yogis denounce the material world. That's because yoga is a very practical scientific method for living a balanced life. It does not denounce anything, but simply calls upon us to consciously inspect how we conduct our actions. That's karma—the law of cause and effect. We must remember that every action in life creates a reaction, just as a mirror reflects an image. If we wish to prosper, we must pay attention to how our thoughts, words, and deeds both create and destroy.

Contrary to what some people may believe, the practice of yoga is not about living in a cave in an impoverished, austere manner. The practice of yoga fully acknowledges the realities of living in a material world. It encourages us to incorporate the four important goals of: soulful growth, meaningful work, pleasure, and wealth into living a fulfilling and meaningful life. Yoga encourages us to prosper while consciously paying attention to how we use our energy.

Lakshmi reminds us that affluence should be respected because in reality, affluence is a forceful stream of energy that has great power. It can create or destroy depending upon how we use it.

In the tradition of Padmini Vidya, wealth is not the accumulation of material things. Wealth is the ability to manipulate the energy of consciousness so as to bring about prosperity. Material things come and go, but once achieved, the consciousness of prosperity is eternal. It becomes our frame of reference and our way of looking and acting within the world.

The material world, on the other hand, is a constant flow of changing energy. Youth changes to old age and day to night, but the consciousness of prosperity, once found and fully understood, is eternal. You carry it with you forever.

To fully understand this energy, we need to follow the four aims, or directions of Lakshmi, as well as learn how to find and use the treasures of life found within the container known as the Nidhi.

Although many people have the determination to create wealth, their attitudes in doing so can greatly influence the outcome. The accumulation of wealth takes more than positive thinking. It is a mindset that seeks to create. But we should remember that inert symbols of affluence are not wealth. Wealth is the byproduct of the energy of prosperity. As you think, speak, and act so you become.

Padmini Vidya reminds us that creation and destruction are powerful forces. Be forewarned: many sacred texts mention

Alakshimi, the evil sister of Lakshmi. With disregard for order, disrespect of nature, and poor hygiene, she will bestow poverty and misfortune upon your house.

If you want to bring prosperity into your life, let the energy of prosperity flow out towards others. Apply the Golden Rule of prosperity: **do not take without giving back.** Those who look out for ways to help others and ways to contribute to the betterment of life without expecting anything in return are sure to prosper. They have found a need and are fulfilling it. This brings wealth in many forms.

The goddess Lakshmi tells us that prosperity has far more to offer us than a beautiful home and a large bank account. Death won't let you take any of these things with you. But abundance of potential energy brought into existence through conscious thought will bring you wealth. You are the source of your wealth. **Whatever you have, increase it. Instead of saying it could be less, say it could be more.** Say "I would like to have this," but do it from a place of consciousness and contentment. Be content with what you have and then reach out for more. Lakshmi gives wealth and success to those who ask with sincerity and are willing to do the work. **The work involves developing conscious awareness of how to use the dynamics of potential energy in complete harmony with the soul's path.** When you combine the infinite force of the soul with the finite source of the material world to create good, anything and everything is possible. This is the pathway to prosperity.

Remember this—the most abundant thing in the universe is energy. Use it wisely. The punja or merits we accumulate as we travel through life are with us from lifetime to lifetime. They define us and are by far our most valuable assets. Money can't buy you happiness, but prosperity can!

Now let's take a look at how to find the four aims in life, how to use them, and then how to discover the treasures of life contained within the Nidhi. This is soul walking the pathway to prosperity.

> Although you may gather a million gold coins,
> upon your death, you cannot take with you
> even one copper penny.
>
> (CHINESE PROVERB)

Now to find the Nidhi (container) and the treasures within.

CHAPTER NINETEEN

The Nidhi – the container that holds the treasures of life

The Nidhi is the container that holds all of life's treasures, known as the nidhis. Once we find the container and learn how to open its lid, we will find that all the treasures are available to each and every one of us, and once found, how we use them will bring us either poverty or prosperity. The nidhis are somewhat shrouded in mystery, but remember, a secret is only a secret until it is revealed. Here is one philosophical interpretation of the nidhi and how to find the nidhis contained within:

A person is drawn to pleasurable objects only when they seem to be real, permanent, and potentiality satisfying. When we understand that all objects in life are not permanent and always subject to change, our minds become calm, and we strive towards higher attainment.

According to the ancient text of Padmini Vidya there are nine obstacles that prevent us from finding the nidhis and nine characteristics or qualities required to discover them. Remove the obstacles and develop the characteristics and you will discover how to use the treasures of life to prosper.

The Nine Obstacles (you can refer back to the chapter on obstacles to review them) are:
1. Ill health
2. Boredom and apathy
3. Doubting self
4. Being scattered and careless
5. Doubting one's progress
6. Uncontrolled cravings and desires
7. Allowing your life to get heavy and to become burnt out
8. Getting caught in the maya—the illusion of life
9. Failing to continue a practice (mastery of anything takes continued practice)

According to the Hindu scriptures, there are nine qualities required to discover the nidhis. Discovering them and how to use them will bring you prosperity.

The Nine Characteristics (refer back to the chapter on characteristics to review them) are:
1. Calmness
2. Self-control
3. Self-withdrawal (reflection)
4. Capacity to endure sorrows and sufferings
5. Sincerity and intellectual appreciation
6. Tranquility gained by constant contemplation
7. Discrimination between right and wrong
8. Unshakeable faith, leading one to attain what might appear unattainable
9. The perfected human living connected to the true self; equally disseminating joy, cheer, and bliss to all

These are indeed the nine qualities every human must attain

to discover the treasures of life. These are what the scriptures of the Vedas and the Upanishads describe as the qualities that once attained lead to nirvana. In the Hindu tradition, "nirvana" means to reunite with the universal soul. The soul can only reach this state after living many lives, and that is why we need to work our karma, because the ultimate wealth, pleasure, harmony, and liberation in life is to find moksha, or freedom; the realization that each soul is here to resolve and solve the mysteries of life and death and you cannot do this until you pay your karmic debt. We are here to overcome the obstacles and build good character. You are known by the content of your character. You are a result of every thought, word, and deed. **So, live your life as you would live it in eternity.**

The habits you form are a result of repeated actions you initiated over lifetimes of experience, be they wise or foolish. In yoga we call this samskara, or the impressions that get inscribed into the mental groove of our being. These grooves are formed by repetitive thoughts, patterns, or habits that get deeper over time. If negative impressions get ingrained, the mental emotional *self* is unable to integrate with the other layers of our *self*—the physical, energetic, higher wisdom, and ultimately bliss. This causes us to be off balance and disconnected. To prosper, we must be fully integrated at our highest level in body, mind, and soul.

Once you establish a pattern, it takes conscious work to dissolve it, or in the case of a positive pattern, constant work to maintain it. It may take lifetimes to work this through. That is the nature of karma. We are on an evolutionary journey from lifetime to lifetime to resolve and transcend our negative karma (patterns) and establish ourselves in maksha: the freedom to simply be in a state of eternal bliss. It is by the force of karma that we are born again and again in an attempt to resolve and complete this journey.

According to karma, ignorance is the source of all suffering, and this suffering is the result of the four patterns of karma that obscure or conceal the truth. Once the truth is revealed, we have the ability to transcend our karma.

The Four Blocks

The first pattern is the karma that **blocks knowledge**. Our knowledge of the world comes about through the five senses. When knowledge is blocked, one cannot see the subtle connection between things and events. It is like the person who is emotionally cruel to their partner and cannot understand why the partner is cold.

The second is the karma that **blocks feelings of joy and grief, pleasure and pain.** This means that you cannot separate the opposing forces of nature. We cannot remove night from day. They both exist as a reflection of the other. Every experience in life can be seen as pleasurable or painful, depending upon how we interpret things. A mosquito bites and you feel the pain of the itch. You scratch the itch and feel the pleasure in scratching. Same bite bringing both pain and pleasure.

The third is the karma that blocks **vitality, longevity, or life span.** The theory of karma states that the longer you live, the more experiences you have, the greater your knowledge, and so the wiser you become. The length of your life is one thing, but the vitality of your life is another. The vitality you have now is a direct result of the last life. Be tremendously enthusiastic about life now and it will affect this life as well as the next life. According to karma, the karma affecting your next life is formed during the last forty-eight minutes of this incarnation.

The fourth karma is that which blocks or **hinders your willpower.** When this kind of karma is operating, it makes us incapable of doing even the simplest of things. This block is grounded in self-doubt. Negative thoughts grow and become more negative, more emotional, and more dangerous. This develops into anxiety, fear, anger, and even hostility. Finally, it breaks out into self-destructive actions. When you lose the ability to harness your willpower many complications will arise in your life.

Master **blocked knowledge, blocked feelings, blocked vitality, unhealthy lifestyle patterns, and the inability to harness your free will** and you will have the tools and the knowledge that will lead you to the nidhis or the treasures of life. But remember, it takes work—that's karma!

Keep the nine obstacles, nine qualities, and the four patterns in mind as we now take a look at the nidhis: the treasures of life.

Then I will show you where to look for the Nidhi (the container) that holds the nidhis. It will then be up to you to find it, open it, and use the treasures within.

What are the nidhis and where can you find them? Follow along.

I hope to be a good teacher by showing you where to look, but not what to see.

CHAPTER TWENTY

The Nidhis— The treasures of life

Sexuality is the First Treasure

Most likely, this first treasure surprised you. The very first thing you are in life is a sexual being. That makes sex a very special treasure. Long before you have a name or an image, you are a sexual being. From the moment of conception your sexuality is formed. Your sex, and then your sexual orientation, define and strongly influence how you live your life. This energy must be harnessed if you are to prosper.

The human mind needs stimuli to fuel its enthusiasm, imagination, and desire. At the top of the list of stimuli is sex. This powerful force can destroy great empires or to build great fortunes. The world is ruled by emotions, not reason, and the emotional desire or drive for sex is the most powerful. Everything in the world is designed to stimulate the sexual urge; to make us feel sexier and more desirable. Take sex away and the world, as we know it, would crumble.

Sex by itself is simply the drive towards procreation and physical gratification, but the treasure of sex is so much more.

The powerful sex drive is the force that gives rise to all of creation. Without the sexual drive, life as we know it would disappear.

Most highly successful people are very sexual. The secret to their success is their ability to turn the sexual energy of charm and charisma into a force that creates prosperity. They understand how to use posture, adornment, and charm to create a powerful force that is so much more than pure physical sexual energy. Sexual energy is a powerful force that must be harnessed and used to create, or if left to run wild it will destroy.

Research tells us that sex is good for our physical health and for clearing the mind. To prosper, calmness and self-control must align with our sexual energy. When this happens, we transform the use of our sexual energy from the drive for pure physical expression and gratification into a highly developed drive toward achieving our goals.

The creative use of sexual energy requires unshakable faith and willpower. The desire for sexual expression is innate and natural. It cannot and should not be suppressed. It should be given a creative outlet that enriches the body, the mind, and the soul. If properly harnessed, the sexual urge will find expression through creative endeavors, and these will bring you prosperity.

How to harness it? Take your mind off the sexual urge and then apply that energy towards your creative endeavors with the same enthusiasm and determination that you would in pursuit of sex.

Creativity is a manifestation of sexual energy. The greatest creative gift to the world is when a soul reincarnates in body and mind for the purpose of bringing forth potential energy. It is about realizing that our personal creativity is rooted in and derived from our sexuality, and how we define it and use it. Therefore, sexuality is a great creative treasure and if used properly will lead to prosperity.

Understanding this, you will then have converted the most powerful drive on Earth into a force that is creatively unbeatable. But it will require **self-control** and **discipline, two characteristics worth developing.** It takes work—that's karma.

Health is the Second Treasure

Right alongside sexuality is your health, for without it everything else in life is meaningless. Your health is your true wealth and the most important thing in the world. Good health is the ultimate treasure of life, for it is with good health that we enjoy all that life has to offer. It is very difficult to enjoy life when you are sick and tired.

Money won't buy you good health, however, prosperity may afford you good food, warm shelter, and good medical care; things that are necessary for good health. Therefore, it is good to live in a prosperous society.

According to karma, your journey on Earth is not about the body and the mind; however, without the body and the mind, the soul cannot experience this Earthly life. The body is the vehicle and the mind is the GPS of the soul. Therefore, it is our responsibility and duty to take care of our health. Eating healthy, exercising, relaxing, reflecting, laughing, and loving are all good for our health.

When the body, the mind, and the soul are in prefect balance, we have perfect health. And when we have perfect health, we have so much more to give to the world. A healthy, balanced human has the vital power to equally disseminate joy, cheer, and bliss to all.

So, value this treasure above all else by taking good care of yourself. **Honor your health, body, mind, and soul,** because,

> "When health is absent wisdom cannot reveal itself, art cannot become manifest, strength cannot be exerted, wealth is useless and reason is powerless."
>
> HEROPHILIES, 300 B.C.

Love is the Third Treasure

Love comes in many shades and in many forms. Romantic love is one kind of love, but love of family, friends, interests, work, and life are aspects of love that will also fill the heart and nourish the soul. Just remember that love is not sex. It is a spiritual experience that touches the soul. Love is a precious treasure that materializes through caring, compassion, and understanding.

Love may come and it may go more than once in your lifetime. No two loves will ever be the same. Romantic love may come with a burst of powerful energy, but it will evaporate and change with time. How love will change is based upon the absence or presence of true love.

So do not think yourself unfortunate if you have loved and lost. Love comes and loves goes without reason or cause. It is whimsical and comes as it will. If it comes enjoy it, and if it must depart, let it go. No amount of fretting and anguishing will bring it back.

Stay unattached, but never indifferent to love. This requires the capacity to endure. For love to endure, it must stay open and be flexible to the endless possibilities and changes of life.

Now if we mix our sexual energy with love its power begins to multiply. Calmness of purpose, judgement, and balance come into play when sex and love become one. When love and devotion are mixed with sex, we create the ultimate pleasurable human experience; the gift of giving and receiving joy. But remember, love and sex, as well as romance, also have a darker side. The troublesome four—envy, jealousy, resentment, and revenge—can turn love into hate and abuse.

Love, like all emotions, is a state of mind capable of taking both creative and destructive paths. When love is mixed with jealousy, envy, revenge, and resentment it takes on a destructive nature. Therefore, we should encourage compassion, understanding, and forgiveness as the dominating thoughts in our mind and remove the destructive ones. The mind thrives on what we feed it. Through the process of self-awareness and willpower we can control the mind, and then whenever a negative thought enters the mind, we will find the power to change it. In love relationships, more than anything, we must constantly remind ourselves to **change the way we look at things, and the way we look at things will change. Don't get caught in the maya.**

Love is one of life's greatest experiences. Love alone will not bring you happiness, but when mixed with sex and romance, we have the ability to move beyond the finite world and into the realm of the infinite soul. Sincerity and intellectual appreciation for the nature of love is needed if we are to truly experience this treasure.

Love also involves devotion. Bhakti yoga, the yoga of devotion, teaches us to devote ourselves to that which we love so that we might discover the true meaning of success. Love, if consciously cultivated, can harmonize and uplift our personal relationships so that they can serve the spiritual process of self-discovery. With this we discover how to disseminate joy, cheer, and bliss to all.

But this takes work, and that is why we are here on Earth; to work our karma. It is said that if you encounter a bad marriage in this lifetime, it is because you brought that energy forward when you reincarnated. It is simply an opportunity to correct and evolve. Consciously work to create true and meaningful love and you will discover one of the great treasures of life.

Here is a story of love and devotion:

In Ireland, there is a church that up until several years ago held the heart of Saint Lawrence, who fought the battle to free Ireland from oppression. Upon his death bed he asked that his heart be taken, encased in a leather case, and placed in Christ Church in Dublin to show his deep devotion and love for his country. Sadly, thieves broke into the church, tore open the case, and stole the heart. All that is left is a broken case. Never steal or break another person's heart. It always leaves an empty painful void. Love is truly a gift. Honor it, cherish it, and protect it.

> "'Tis better to have loved and lost than
> to have never loved at all."
>
> -ALFRED TENNYSSON

Ethics and Morals are the Fourth Treasure

There are three things humans need in order to both survive and thrive. The first is material goods, including shelter and food. The second is erotic practice, or sex, to ensure the continuation of the species. And the third is rules of behavior, or ethical and moral codes of conduct.

Ethics are morals in action. Morals are knowing the difference between right and wrong and choosing right. Ethics is morally acting in such a way as to bring the greatest good for the greatest many. It is important that we develop the ability to discriminate between what is right and what is wrong. The underlying factor is to **do no harm.**

An ethic is a code or a rule created by an individual or an organization to establish standards of conduct. Therefore, "ethics" are sets of these codes or rules. At the same time, ethics also refers to the study, or branch of knowledge, that deals with moral principles.

What, then, are morals?

Morals refer to an individual's personal beliefs about what is right and wrong. The word *moral* can also refer to a lesson concerning what is right or wrong that can be derived from a story or other experience. But for prosperity, morals can best be understood as the personal standards from which we choose what is acceptable and what is unacceptable behavior.

Ethics lay the foundation for the choices we make. Morals lay the foundation for the ethics we establish. Without morals, we would have no ethics, and since it is well understood that different people often abide by different ethics, this begs the question: Where do our morals come from? Where is there justice?

All humans desire, survival, long life, knowledge, justice, fame, love, and salvation. As far as we know, all other living things only seek survival. Therefore, the successful survival and thriving of the human species is based upon good morals and ethics. Make the wrong choice and there will be consequences;

that's karma—*life becomes what life does*. You must decide what is right and what is wrong. No one can do this for you. How and what we choose reflects what we value.

Without food, clothing, and shelter the body becomes weak. Without love and sex, the mind becomes restless and unsatisfied. Without morals and ethics, the conscience goes astray.

In difficult times, people tend to lose their faith and resort to shortcuts and questionable practices. In this worldly life they may seem to succeed with these tactics, but in the end, they will leave deep scars on their consciousness and influence the course of their future lives in adverse ways.

Character, good behavior, commitment to truth, and mental and physical purity are essential in this life, especially in trying times, if you wish to truly prosper.

From a humanistic point of view, it is good to make money and enjoy the pleasures of life. However, when people are only attached to money and pleasure without a moral and ethical underpinning, overindulging in the decadence of the world is inevitable. When profit and pleasure are guided by ethics and morals, they become instruments for humanitarian and soulful growth. It is good to make a profit, just do it from a consciously-guided place.

While our modern-day culture encourages us to get rich no matter what the cost, yoga challenges us to look at money as a divine force that we must handle responsibly. We are encouraged to earn a good living and even to become rich. However, the path must be honest and lawful. We must always seek to do no harm and do the greatest good for the greatest many.

Karma reminds us that our first responsibility is to take care of ourselves, then our family and friends, and then the world at large; never forgetting to take time for soulful pursuit.

Self-awareness and self-reflection are often needed when deciding how best to go about meeting our responsibilities.

Some people think the desire to fulfill our inner life makes it difficult to make money. This is not true. When we do things with a clear conscious, prosperity is sure to come. Just remind yourself that money and wealth have the power to do more than poverty. So, seek wealth and enjoy the pleasures of life based upon good morals and ethics.

Sex, wealth, and ethics are the cornerstones of a civilized society. Just as your soul needs to be fed pure energy, the conscience needs ethics, the mind love and sex, and the body wellbeing. Without these three things, life begins to crumble. The measure of success or failure in life is the degree of your happiness and not the size of your bank account. However, fulfilling the desire for wealth based upon reputable morals and ethics will lead to prosperity.

Remember this: humans desire long life, knowledge, justice, fame, love, and salvation. All other life forms, as far as we know, only seek to survive. The successful survival and thriving of human beings are based upon good morals and ethics. This is a treasure of great importance. **Act ethically from this moral base; do unto others as you would have them do unto you. Do no harm and always seek to do the greatest good for the greatest many.**

Potential is the Fifth Treasure

Potential energy, unlike kinetic energy, which is energy in motion, is stored energy that exists by virtue of its relative position to everything else in the universe. Just by your existence in relationship to everything else in the world, you have been given the treasure of potential energy. That means you have the potential to create, and your potential is only limited by how you position yourself in relationship to everything else in the world. Self-acceptance is fundamental to discovering your potential. You are who you are so you should make the best of it. Don't compare yourself or your life to others. Instead, encourage yourself to attain your highest potential. Life is abundant with potential energy. Realize this and you will never go without.

The laws of thermodynamics tell us that energy is never lost. It simply changes form. Padmini Vidya, as a science, tells us that when we consciously create and release a particular desire, the energy of that desire manifests into material form. But be careful because consciousness has the potential to create or destroy. This is not a "think positive" proposition. It is about giving a thought the potential to manifest. Nothing in life is created without first some level of conscious energy. This requires that you have faith and a belief that you can attain what you desire through the use of your potential energy.

Nothing can exist that doesn't doesn't already exist as potential energy. We could never travel to faraway lands if the potential to do so was not already there. We, as humans, have the potential to create on a very high level. Our brains allow us to master the complexities of life. An insect, on the other hand, is limited. But it does have wings and can fly. It's biomechanically designed to do so. However, the creative potential of our brains has allowed us to build flying machines, and now we can fly. Who knows, perhaps someday an insect will develop the potential energy needed to save the world!

Potential energy is not simply positive thinking or mind over matter. However, potential energy is best served with a positive outlook. Potential exists everywhere, and it is up to us to turn it into kinetic energy, or material form. If your energy is negative, you will draw negative destructive energy towards you. Alashimi, the evil sister of Lakshmi, might visit you and wreak havoc on your house.

If you are positive, you will draw positive energy towards you. For example, people are drawn to a smile. This is essential if you wish to prosper. No one ever prospers in a place of negative energy for very long.

For life to exist at all, there must be potential energy. Even science tells us that for the material world to exist there must be the potential. Consciousness needs a vehicle, such as the brain, to bring thoughts into material manifestation. But it needs nothing to exist. It is potential waiting to materialize through its relationship to everything else in the universe.

Every thought, word, and deed are a manifestation of potential energy. But for potential energy to bring you prosperity, it must follow the success formula: have a **vision** + backed with **desire** + a well-thought-out **plan** + **persistent and consistent action** = **success.**

Dreams and desires are a part of life. Even aimless people aspire for things. However, not all people have clear and concise goals, but everyone harbors vague ideas about their future, where they want to go, what they want to do, and how to become prosperous and happy. Most people want to help their children and family succeed in life. In the end, only a few manage to reach their goals. What contributes to their success is persistency and consistency, with a clear vision, a well-thought-out plan, and a burning desire to succeed.

You have been given potential energy as a gifted treasure. It is very powerful, but useless without conscious thought and action to bring it to fruition. Potential is everywhere. Realize this and you will prosper.

Courage is the Sixth Treasure

Courage is seen as an attribute of good character and is respected. We equate it to a mighty warrior or someone who goes to battle. Yet courage is not just about physical bravery. Courage also means the ability to speak out against injustice, to take a risk in the face of adversity, to open yourself up to the vulnerabilities of life, and to believe in your convictions even when met with mockery and contempt.

Nothing in life is ever accomplished without a dose of courage. That's because courage is the engine of ingenuity. Attempt something new and above the mediocracy of everyday life and you will be met with opposition, criticism, and ridicule. Rise above this, solider onward, and you will discover the treasure of courage.

It takes courage to forgive, to be humble, and to be respectful and compassionate in a world that equates courage with brute force and domination. It takes courage to speak your mind and be true to yourself when faced with conformity. It takes courage to love and be open to vulnerability.

Courage, therefore, is the ability to remain strong within yourself even when the outside world is nebulous and moving. But the greatest use of courage is to overcome *dis-couragement*. Courage is the only antidote for failure and disappointment. To develop the capacity to endure suffering and hardships requires both faith and courage.

Our fiercest enemy is the ego. It is a mighty force and not easy to control. It takes courage to look within and find the strength to successfully manage the challenges of life. Courage requires nothing more than simply letting go of fear while holding on to unfathomable and unshakable faith and believing in yourself. Remove fear and the warrior within you will stand courageous rather than as a hapless victim. Thus, the warrior with courage conquers all.

> Courage is not the absence of fear;
> it is the conquest of it.
>
> WILLIAM DANFORTH (1870-1955)

Power is the Seventh Treasure

Power is referred to as the ability to influence the will or conduct of others. It is also the ability to control and direct your energy towards your goals, as well as control over your conduct. Power resides within the individual. It is independent and informal in nature and is derived from charisma and status. Power allows a person to influence and set an example for millions of people. On a smaller scale, we have power over our children, employees, students, family members, friends, and ourselves. How we use power determines our prosperity.

Power has nothing to do with accumulating great material wealth. However, oftentimes great wealth comes as the result of this treasure. Misuse of power is known as manipulation. It may gain you the upper hand temporarily, but it will at some point bring rebellion, disgust, hatred, humiliation, and destruction. Think of all the powerful leaders who misused their power. Most were eventually met with great opposition, defeat, and death. Power at its best is used to empower yourself, as well as others, towards making the world a better place.

Power is a mighty force. Whether we believe it or not, we all have power. We have the power to persuade, to direct, to dominate, to master, and to teach. In all our relationships within the world, we have the power to do good deeds and to act unselfishly or to manipulate and control. If power is attained without the right moral and ethical underpinning, it can become a destructive force justified by selfish means.

According to yoga, the world began as un-manifested pure consciousness. Everything that was ever to be was one connected force of energy. When the universe began to manifest, the ego was born, then the individual, and then the mind. From the mind arrived the gross physical world. As we think, so our world exists. This is the power of life. It is called free will.

What we see outside of our selves is our manifestation of the physical world. But what we must always remember is that it is the nature of life to evolve and dissolve. When we lose the process of evolution and live in the fear of dissolution, power has the potential to corrupt.

Evolution is more than just a Darwinian theory. It is about consciousness.

A parent guides a child with a strong sense of wrong and right based upon honesty and openness. This is power at its best. We help a friend to make a decision by lending our support. We teach each other how to be good partners in a relationship. All of these involve teaching, guiding, directing, and even persuading and dominating. It's all about the intent and how that intent is directed. That is the beauty of power. Like the expansion and contraction of our breath, life has a natural rhythm of exchange. When power is exchanged with compassion and love, our thoughts, words, and deeds align with our sense of right and wrong.

Now, knowing that you can create your own reality is a very powerful thought. Add to this the power we all have to influence, sway, coach, and instruct and we can see how important it is that power is used for good. If a friend asks your opinion about taking a new job, or needs a little support when it comes to a love interest, are you able to guide them unselfishly? You have just gotten a promotion and are now in charge of other people. Do you treat them fairly, or are you overcome with a sense of misguided power and seek to rule rather than lead? Power may bring great wealth. Do you use it to buy and control other people, or do you use it to help other people excel?

These are moral and ethical questions that sit at the base of your power. When power comes from a base of love, compassion, and understanding, there is always the right moral and ethical guidepost to assist us with our decisions. When we see the world as an interconnected web of energy, we realize that to hurt even one small fragment of life is to hurt all of it. Here we begin to understand the great force of power known as supreme consciousness. To hurt and destroy anyone or anything would be to hurt and destroy the whole.

If you wish to proper, do not give away your power and do not abuse it. As Sri Chimnoy reminded us,

> "The day the power of love overrules the love of power, the world will know peace."

Remember: as you think, say, and do, so your life becomes. Examine the power of your intentions and then seek to do the greatest good for the greatest many. In this, your power will evolve and it will always be used for good. The characteristics of self-control and sincere intellectual appreciation are required to discover the treasure of power.

Authority is the Eighth Treasure

Authority means to have the power or right to give orders, to make decisions, and to enforce rules of order. This is truly a treasure of great importance, for it has the power to create or destroy depending upon one's moral and ethical underpinning.

Just remember that orders, decisions, and rules of conduct based upon good and sound morals and ethics is the basis of a prosperous society.

We all have some level of authority. Mostly it is the authority we have over our own conduct; our perception and attitudes. How we decide and enforce our conduct may run counter to our moral and ethical point of view. So, although we often think of authority as someone with great power, it is a treasure we all share.

Authority means the power to make and implement rules of order. Whether it is the head of a household or the head of a nation, their rules must be followed. Leaders must lead and people must follow proper modes of conduct if any group, small or large, is to prosper. The problems happen when authority and power are misused because of greed, deceit, anger, and pride. The four great passions will lead to destruction if not tethered by ethical and moral codes of conduct. Never forget that life has a perfect accounting system. Nothing goes unbalanced or unnoticed. The laws of karma state that for every effect there will be a cause. *Life becomes what life does.*

Authority brings with it a great responsibility. Someone

of great authority is often known as an expert and therefore holds great knowledge. This knowledge often grants power, prestige, and position. Authority also means to have the legal and formal rights to give orders and make decisions. How we use this authority determines whether a person, family, group, or society prospers, or not.

Just remember, we all have the treasure of authority. Every day we make decisions and enforce rules of order. The moral duty of anyone in a place of power and authority is to make the world a better place by making those who they have power and authority over healthy, happy, and safe. Their happiness and welfare then becomes the leader's happiness and welfare. When this happens, everyone prospers. Sincerity and appreciation are required to discover this treasure. Authority is truly a great treasure. Use it wisely and you will prosper.

Tenacity is the Ninth Treasure

Through tenacity we learn to apply potential energy persistently and consistently to our endeavors. Without it nothing will be achieved. Tenacity is at the head of the list when it comes to the use of potential energy.

Without the ability to endure hardships and suffering, nothing is achieved. Success is impossible unless you have the willpower and determination to move past hurdles and difficulties. Tenacity is the ability to not give up, even when met with defeat. It is an intuitive understanding that defeat is only temporary. The ability to keep marching through all of life's ups and downs is the mark of a tenacious person. In yoga, it is said that without the ability to endure great hardships self-discipline cannot be attained and character cannot be built. Without self-discipline, contentment and happiness are impossible. Without contentment and happiness, it is impossible to prosper. It is through tenacity that a person unleashes the potential energy to attain the unattainable.

Humor is the Tenth Treasure

Never lose your sense of humor! Laughter is a great sound—that's why we've all heard the saying, "Laughter is the best medicine."

There is strong evidence that laughter can improvehealth and help fight disease. Laughter improves immune functioning, outlook, mood, and emotions while reducing stress. Studies also show that people with a good sense of humor live longer.

Humor (laughter) exists in all cultures and at all ages. It is an essential and fundamental part of human behavior. Humor can be used to make people feel good, to gain intimacy, and to help us cope with stress. A sense of humor helps us to form connections to the world and provides meaning to our life. Humor also correlates with learning, wisdom, and emotional well-being.

The key to a happy life is to laugh and make others laugh without mocking, ridiculing, or hurting anyone. It is also the ability to laugh at yourself and the absurdities of life. Self-acceptance of your own idiosyncrasies is the key to a happier and more joyful life. Find the humor in all of life and you will discover the power of laughter. To me, the most beautiful sound in the world is to hear the ones I love laughing. I know in those moments they are experiencing pleasure; one of the great aims in life. A sincere and intellectual appreciation for life will keep you laughing.

Maya means illusion or boundaries, and because of the maya we are all bound by the material world. Remember it is not the world that is an illusion. It is our perception of it. The world is made up of real experiences through which we gain real knowledge into the nature of our true self. Our sense of humor is part of our true nature and is an integral part of how we see the world.

Life will present you with many challenges. Each of these will test your resilience. If you cannot laugh at yourself and at the craziness of life, you will lose two of the great pleasures of life; laughter and a sense of humor. **Never lose it! It's a great treasure.**

> "If we couldn't laugh, we would all go insane?"
> JIMMY BUFFETT

Beauty is the Eleventh Treasure

Beauty is in the eyes and the heart of the beholder, or simply put; the beauty of the world is within you. Beauty is not found in an image, but in how we see the world. **Beauty is as much about attitude** as it is about the physical body. Good grooming, exercise, and a healthy diet will help, but not if we are burdened with a negative attitude. Enlightenment, happiness, and self-love are all conducive to finding beauty.

What destroys beauty? Fear! All the great pleasures of life bring with them the fear of losing them. Beauty is one of those things. It's alright to have a beautiful face and a beautiful body. The problem comes when we fear losing them. That's when vanity and ego come into play.

Vanity and the ego can blur the line between real beauty and the perception of beauty.

In most religious teachings, **vanity** is considered to be self-centered and a form of self-idolatry. It means to consider oneself of great importance. Philosophically, vanity is referred to as the **ego or pride**. Nietzsche wrote in *Beyond Good and Evil*, "Vanity is fear of appearing original; it is thus a lack of pride, but not necessarily a lack of originality." Mason Cooley in one of his aphorisms wrote, **"Vanity well fed is benevolent. Vanity hungry is spiteful."**

It is this last quote that blurs the line between vanity, the ego, and real beauty.

Show me a person who does not see and appreciate beauty and I will show you a spiteful and angry soul. But show me a person, who sees, lives, and believes in **beauty** and I will show you a **benevolent being**.

Beauty, like all of life, comes in different forms. It is **physical** and material, it is conceptual and **mindful,** and it is ethereal and **soulful.** Mostly, we are drawn to physical beauty by conceptually deciding what is and what is not beautiful to us. We then hope to hold onto what we believe to be the permanent and satisfying aspect of beauty. But with all things in life, we must appreciate that beauty is continually changing. The physical beauty of youth gives way to an inner beauty that can only be gained through maturity. The blossom of a fruit is beautiful, but it is only when it changes, ages, and ripens that it becomes life-sustaining and sweet fruit. Understanding this brings calmness of mind, and with calmness of mind we become poised, tranquil, and contemplative. **Here we have the opportunity to develop a sincere and intellectual appreciation for beauty.**

A beautiful thought is to see beauty where there is ugliness. To see the good where there is bad. This is not a naïve Pollyanna approach to life, but rather the realization that beauty

The Nidhis— The treasures of life

is **found in symmetry and in contrast**. For example: you see a horrible ugly crime, like the Boston Marathon bombing or 9-11 World Trade Center attack, but with this horror comes the comforting and caring for those who are grieving. This touches **the beauty of humanity**.

Beautiful thoughts are the ones that always come from a place of love, kindness, caring, and respect. **Nothing beautiful can come** from thoughts that are hateful, malicious, and deceitful. Just like everything in life, beautiful thoughts are only reflected by their similarity and their contrast.

Karma reminds us that our thoughts are pure. We give them emotion. Emotions affect your aura, or your energy shield, and your aura reflects the beauty, or lack of beauty, in your body, mind, and soul. Remember, you are what you think, say, and do. So, think, speak, and do beautiful things, because **a world without beauty would be a placid, ugly, and indistinguishable place.**

Beauty is one of the great treasures of life. It has nothing to do with attributes and adjectives and everything to do with understanding the true nature of beauty. It is the ability to live fully, embracing each moment with joy. When you walk through life with calmness, contemplation, and appreciation for all of life, you will find beauty everywhere. But mostly you will find beauty within yourself.

The world is real and full of beauty. The maya (illusion) is in your perception and interpretation of things. Whether you see the world as beautiful or ugly is all up to you. It's all about your free will—believing in the power of choice. To see the beauty of life is truly a treasure and sure to bring you prosperity.

> "Beauty is not an image. It's a proclivity
> embedded in your soul. Practice self-control
> along with an intellectual and sincere
> appreciation or life. Look within and
> you will find beauty everywhere."
>
> DOCTOR LYNN

Happiness is the Twelfth Treasure

Of all of life's emotional gifts, happiness might just be the most treasured gift of all.

Happiness means to be content with what you have while having the confidence to know you have the potential, the power, and the courage to reach out and be so much more. Everyone wants to be happy, and yet happiness often eludes most of us. So, if we all want happiness, why are we unhappy? Most likely because we feel we got less than we expected. With expectations comes disappointment, and that leads to unhappiness.

What is happiness? True happiness is simply pure joyful energy that harmoniously flows through space and time. Think of a place and a time when you were happy. How did it make you feel? That is the energy flow of the treasure of happiness. Once you discover that you are the source of your own happiness, instead of your expectations, happiness will be with you forever.

The thing to **remember** about happiness is that **life is ever-changing**. Nothing is permanent except that which you cultivate within. In the Hindu practice, Lord Shiva is the King of the Dance of Life. Shiva is portrayed as the force of destructive energy that lays the foundation for creation. Shiva dances at the cosmic wheel of life surrounded by a ring of fire, which symbolizes the eternal cycles of birth, life, and death. The name Shiva means **liberation,** or the freedom to dance and express oneself. He cannot stop time from passing or things from changing, but he can find happiness and bliss amid the chaos of life. To find happiness, **keep dancing!**

In yoga, there is a pose called the **prosperous pose,** or lotus pose. It is also called the **happy pose.** In Sanskrit, it means the swirling motion of a cross symbolizing the spinning of creation and evolution. It means that happiness is **created within and then evolves outward into our** intellectual view of the world and is then present in how we move through the world; be it graceful or awkward. Happiness manifests as **"the sweet nectar"** or the **molecules** within our brain's chemistry called endorphins. These molecules of happiness may take us on a euphoric ride where we begin to experience **bliss in the body, mind, and soul.**

With calmness of being, happiness becomes contagious. A happy soul brings joy, good cheer, and bliss to everyone and everything they encounter. Prosperity is drawn to happiness just like we are drawn to happy people.

Happiness is as basic a need as food and water. Ask anyone what they would want most in life and most likely, right after good health, they will choose happiness.

There is a fable about a musk deer that best describes our search for happiness. The fabled musk deer has a scented spot above its forehead that gives off the scent of musk. The deer is intensely attracted to the scent of the musk and so runs here and there in search of it, not realizing that the scent is on its forehead. Happiness is like that. We run here and there in search of it, never realizing that happiness is within us and not somewhere out there.

To find happiness, stop anguishing. It never solved anything. Anguish only brings pain, stress, and ill health. Approach the world with selfless motives. Know that you are the source (potential) of your own happiness. Stop expecting and start enjoying life and you will see a very different world. You will begin to use the world for a very different purpose, and that will bring you happiness. Remember: the greatest amount of negative karma goes into destroying happiness and joy. *Change the way you look at things and the way you see things will change.*

Abraham Maslow, in Maslow's Hierarchy of Needs, referred to the hierarchy of needs as the motivational force of the individual; the highest being **self-actualization.** This highest need may hold the key to happiness. To be self-actualized simply means to grow whole, and to grow whole means to reach the pinnacle of completeness. Nothing more is needed, and therefore one finds the contentment and satisfaction that leads to happiness. The self-actualized human moves with poise, tranquility, grace, and ease.

Happiness requires contentment. Be content with what you have and then reach out to create more. This is how we prosper, succeed, and become wealthy. Contentment is one of the goals of yoga and one of the most difficult things for us to attain. There is a natural tendency for humans to want more. Even when we experience happiness, we want more happiness.

Contentment means to be happy with what you have and not desire that which you have not earned. **Jean Paul Sartre said, "Happiness is not doing what you want, but wanting what you do."**

Happiness requires discipline and self-control. **Even the moments of unhappiness that we wish never transpired** can bring us happiness. No one wants to go through a divorce, a strained relationship, loss of a loved one, loss of a job, or any other disappointment in life. But when we see these things as simply a part of the big picture of life, we intuitively know it is best to let go and let be. Observe life. Be content with what comes into and goes out of your life, and you will find happiness.

How can we be happy when we are sad, hurt, angry, and alone? All the seeds of life's emotions and feelings are within us. **What we feed these emotions and feelings is what will manifest.** So, if we feed sorrow with sorrow, sorrow will manifest. But if we feed sorrow with happiness before long happiness will be your state of being. **That is the whole point to happiness.** It is within us, and we alone have the power to be happy no matter what the circumstances. Happiness then is about self-realization; realize you have the power to self-control and direct your life.

Money and material gain won't buy happiness. Those things of the world come and go. But remember this: happiness does not come without work. You must earn your punja (good merits) and remove your papa (bad deeds) to discover happiness. **We must work diligently** to release ourselves from the bonds of the ego and lift ourselves to a higher level of consciousness where we realize that it is our inner source and not the desires of the ego that bring us **true happiness.**

Did you know that happiness is only a thought away? Positive psychology research indicates that thinking three to five gratitude thoughts a day improves the immune system and boosts happiness. Gratitude fills the soul with joy.

Be Grateful

Be grateful that you don't already have everything you want
There's more to come!

Be grateful for your health
It is your true wealth

Be grateful for the simple things
Food, shelter, and warmth
Be grateful for the sunrise
It brings you a new day
Be Grateful for your friends
They are your greatest support
Be grateful for what you have
Count your blessings

Next time you feel happy, stop and observe the feeling. **Capture it and become aware of how easy it is to apply it to your life.** Remember this: in life it is better to be happy than righteous. Righteous people only see the hard and fast fist of the ego. They hold onto desires, expectations, and notions of possessing when in fact **we own nothing**, not even our bodies. The body is only on loan for this short walk on Earth called life. Be grateful and good to yourself, and you will **be happy.**

Understanding this, you will find contentment. Then, when you **ask yourself "who am I?"** the answer will be, **"I am happy."**

Be the source of your own happiness, because it is truly a gift to be treasured. Be mindful of each step you take along the pathway of life, and each step will be an end in itself. With no distinction between the journey and the destination, you will discover that happiness is not a destination. It is here right now—just like the musk deer—right in your head. Be mindful ~ Be happy!

From the movie: *Café Society*, directed by Woody

> "Live life every day as if it is your last day, and one day you'll be right."

Now the Thirteenth Treasure….

There is an essence that exists everywhere, and yet at times can be hard to obtain. However, this essence is available to everyone. It can be as hard and unrelenting as rock, and yet agile and yielding. It is both loved and despised. We call it **free will**. Next to a healthy life, free will is the most precious treasure of all. We all have been given free will, and yet few souls understand it or know how it works. Through will and will alone humans have overcome tremendous odds. It gives us the capacity to endure sorrows and suffering. It is the power to consciously choose and control the force of our energy towards a particular desire. To will is to have faith in the ability to transform the ordinary into the extraordinary. It is akin to tenacity—the ability to hold on with deep determination. It is based in an **unshakable faith** that allows anyone who understands it the ability to **attain** whatever they desire.

Free will is the unrelenting ability to direct your life towards a desired end. We can use it to change every level of our reality. We are only limited by the boundaries we choose. Every moment we are presented with choices that allow us to define and redefine who and what we choose to be. We call this thinking. Karma yoga teaches us that there are no right or wrong thoughts, words, or actions, only consequences.

You are defined by what you let occupy the space within your mind. You are what you think and not because you think. You control your thoughts through the exercise of free will. Understanding how to turn self-destructive negative thoughts into positive self-enforcing thoughts is how to use free will constructively and how we prosper. How do you do this?

Remember, as you think you become. You have the power of **self-control**. *Pay attention to what you let occupy your mind because what occupies your mind occupies you.* The greatest use of free will is to consciously choose to bring **health, happiness, and peace** to the world. This is the treasure that leads to *moska*, or liberation.

These are the thirteen treasures of life known as the nidhis. But where do we find them?

CHAPTER TWENTY-ONE

Where are the Nidhis?

The treasurers of life are available for everyone. You just need to reach into the container that holds the treasures and use them wisely. Where do you find the container? Here the secret is revealed: **YOU are the container, and you hold all the treasures of life.** Use them wisely.

Some people will find it easy to manipulate these intangible treasures into vast assets and others may need to concentrate intensely. It will require the ability to endure, appreciate, contemplate, and have faith. Be calm, use self-control, look within, and you will discover all the treasures and how to use them to become the master of your own life. Rule wisely.

Prosperity is not the accumulation of material things; it is the active and willful manipulation of the energy of consciousness that creates prosperity. It is not static. It is active abundant potential energy available to everyone. You just need to discover how to tap into it, and then how to direct it towards prosperity. As you think, say, and do, so you become. *Life becomes what life does.*

Now you are Soul Walking and on the path to prosperity.

When all of the obstacles that impede your soul are overcome, awareness is achieved and the soul is released from the power of karma. It is here that we prosper by engaging our free will to use our potential energy and courage, ethically and morally, with power and authority, humor, and respect to create love, beauty, and health. Here you prosper.

Pay attention to your karma. Be careful not to **fall into D-GAP**. Deceit, greed, anger, and pride will not bring you peace and happiness. Work your karma diligently to remove D-GAP by adhering to the suggested ways of conduct. Remember: **you can change 84 percent of your karma.**

Consciously work to master the **Troublesome Four. Envy, jealousy, resentment, and revenge** will overshadow the beauty in the world. *Have compassion and forgive; everyone is here on Earth doing the best they can.*

Be persistent and be careful with what you let occupy your mind. It will occupy you. Be patient; all things are difficult before they become easy. Keep your focus on the four aims in life: **wealth, pleasure, harmony, and liberation.** These will lead to prosperity. Every day ask Lakshmi to direct you towards the four aims. Then at the end of the day reflect upon how they came to you. If you ask for them with sincerity, you will find them. Don't look for the "big" things. Look for the small things and you will begin to learn how to prosper every day of your life.

The potential to create wealth exists everywhere. Just keep an eye out for the time gates; the opportunities that exist all around you. When you find them, use the power of your courage to stay focused. Then, keep moving forward, shifting your view from wealth to prosperity. Focus on what you can do to make the world a better place and then do it. Everyone will prosper and you will become wealthy.

Wealth is the manifestation of divine energy, and this energy must be honored. Wealth if misused will eventually bring Alakshmi the evil sister of Lakshmi; she will rain destruction and poverty upon you. When wealth comes to you, no matter how big or how small, remember that it can rise very fast, but if you are not careful the fall to poverty will be even faster. So, if wealth comes to you use it wisely. Never take without giving something back.

Everything in life must sacrifice. For every gain there is always a loss. A tree blooms. Then its blossoms give way to bearing fruit and then the tree sacrifices its fruit to nourish the earth.

True prosperity can never be achieved when we have more than our share at the expense of others. That's where good ethics and morals come into play. Use these two treasures together and you will prosper. Just remember wealth is not about possessions, but about an active flow of energy that benefits all of life. Dwell in a state of prosperity and you will dwell in a conscious state of wealth energy. But this is more than pure positive thinking. This stream of energy can reshape your life in either positive or negative ways depending upon how you use it. Wealth can bestow great power while misuse will surely make a person suffer.

Wealth, in its most perfect form, equally disseminates health, happiness, and peace to all.

Wealth can mean a lot of things, such as good health, great friends, a loving family, and a comfortable life. When food, shelter, health, the arts, education, and pleasure coexist with good ethics and morals, true wealth is achieved. **Be generous and count your blessings.**

Be humble. The real measure of wealth is not found in the size of your bank account; it is found in the degree of your happiness.

> "Happiness is not doing what you want,
> but wanting what you do."
>
> JEAN PAUL SARTRE

We are hardwired for pleasure. It is an innate human drive so we should not try to suppress it. The key to pleasure is aiming it in the right direction and never taking it to extremes. It is pleasurable to enjoy good food, have a comfortable home, and to enjoy travel, art, music, love, and beautiful things of the material world. Just see them for what they are; an opportunity to experience pleasure and joy. In and of themselves they are simply objects. We add emotions and feelings.

Each day get up and aim to bring pleasure into your life, and then take a moment to be grateful for the experience. You will soon discover how and where to find pleasure and happiness, and this will lead to a prosperous life, for after good health, the happiness that comes from finding pleasure in your life is one of life's greatest treasures. It is not pleasure that destroys the good; it is greed.

Harmony is the key to balance and balance is the key to living a prosperous life. Harmony is the ability to create a peaceful flow of energy.

To create harmony, seek balance in all things, and in all things find balance.

Liberate yourself by letting go of the things you cannot change or control. Remember, there are only two things in life you cannot change: your individuality and your family of origin. Liberation means to be unattached but not indifferent to the ever-flowing energy of life. It is our expectations and our clinging to certainty that is at the heart of our problems.

Remember, the whole material universe consists of five everlasting and imperishable substances: space, motion, rest, matter, and soul. How you relate to the world matters. Reach into the container of life and make good use of its valuable treasures.

The world is real and here for you to use. **It is your perception and not the world that is the illusion.** So, pay attention to your attitude and how you perceive life. *Change the way you look at things and the way you see things will change.*

The journey is not about your body or your mind, but about the evolution of your soul. Walk with your soul, here and now, and you will discover the pathway to prosperity. **You never step into the same river twice—choose wisely, walk softly, and stay on the path.**

Live each day as you would live it in eternity.

Apply the formula for success: Vison + desire + plan + consistency + persistency = success. All of this must be backed with a positive stream of prosperity consciousness.

Make punja (merits) by giving more than you take. Remember that *poverty is not a virtue, but it can be an inspiration. Live a prosperous life and you will be wealthy.*

Relationships matter. They are the glue that keep us connected to life.

But they will challenge us. **See them as opportunities to evolve.** Always trust yourself: **trust is the union of intelligence (knowing, understanding, and compassion) and integrity. Ignorance and deceit are its counter opposites.**

Above all else honor your health, for it is truly your wealth.

> "When health is absent, wisdom cannot reveal itself, art cannot become manifest, strength cannot be exerted, wealth is useless, and reason is powerless."
>
> HEROPHILIES, 300 B.C. DIET FOR A NEW AMERICA

Be grateful for all that comes into your life. Being grateful you move though life with a sense of self-control, self-awareness, tranquility, and grace. This is how you prosper.

Remember this: wisdom is in knowing the right path to walk. Integrity is walking it. Walk your soulful path wholly and stay undivided.

You are now **Soul Walking** and on the prosperous path. You are in possession of the treasures of life, and you know where to find them. **You are the container of these treasures. Use them wisely.**

Don't confuse the map for the territory. The map might direct you from here to there, but it will never provide the experience, activity, and knowledge you will discover on the journey. But do use the map as a guide along with your courage to step into the potential abundance of life.

Now come along and begin the journey. You have your purpose, you know your karma, you have your moral compass, and you now know where to find the treasures of life and how to use them. Use them wisely and you will prosper with a purpose.

Karma and Padmini Vidya Yoga are very different than Western modes of thinking. **Their goal is to bring about a conscious realization of the answer to this question:**

> "Soul Walker what do you seek . . . since this world is not your final resting place?"
>
> ANONYMOUS

Let me close with a poem by Guillaume Apollinaire:

"Come to the edge," he said.
"We can't, we're afraid!" they responded.
"Come to the edge," he said.
"We can't, we will fall!" they responded.
"Come to the edge," he said.
And so they came.
And he pushed them.
And they flew.

And if you need a little push to help you stay on the soulful path of prosperity, here is something you can copy and read to yourself every day:

Each day I awake to a perfect day. Let me aim to find within each day wealth, pleasure, harmony, and liberation. My job is to bring to the day health in body, mind, and soul, sexual allure, passion, love, harmony, beauty, humor, compassion, happiness, wisdom, and peace, no matter what the day brings to me. Now I have a purpose and now I am soul walking. I am a prosperous soul with a purpose. Life becomes what life does.

Namaste—I celebrate the path where our souls have met. May you always walk the soulful path with health, happiness, and peace.

Doctor Lynn

For more about Doctor Lynn and her other books:

http://www.doctorlynn.com
http://www.facebook.com/DrLynnAnderson
http://doctorlynnanderson.blogspot.com/

Glossary of Karmic Words and Terms

A

Anna Mayer: The yoga path of healthy eating

G

Gunas: One of the qualities of nature. There are three: sattva, rajas, tamas or balance, activity, and inertia.

K

Karma: A yoga philosophy: action and reaction; cause and effect
Kriya: Balance

L

Lakshimi: Goddess of prosperity

M

Moksha: Liberation
Maya: Illusion

N

Nidhi: Container of treasures
Niyamas: Moral guidepost to observe; purty, contentment. Austerity, self-study, centering on a higher power.

P

Padmini Vidja: The yoga philosophy of prosperity
Papa: Sinful action that leads to wrongdoing or evil
Punja: Right action or deeds that leads to good
Purusha: The divine self that resides in all beings

S

Self: Your essence that always remains stable—true self—soul
Shakti: Vibrant power, vitality, and energy

Y

Yamas: Moral guidepost to abstain from; violence, untruthfulness, stealing, uncontrolled sense, greed

Z

Zen: A philosophy being mindfully present in the moment

www.ingramcontent.com/pod-product-compliance
Lightning Source LLC
LaVergne TN
LVHW012018060526
838201LV00061B/4361